FAMILY iD --- Intentional Direction

Discover Your Family's Unique Purpose and Passion

by
Greg C. Gunn

Foreword by
Craig Groeschel

www.Family-iD.com

BeyondYourManuscript.com

ISBN-13: 9780615586908

ISBN-10: 0615586902

Dedication

I dedicate this book as a promise to our future generations, to pass a clearer, better defined, more powerful vision to every generation. Without it; we will perish from the earth.

I will also be your standard bearer according to our family scripture: Praise the LORD! Happy is the person who honors the LORD, who takes pleasure in obeying his commands. The good man's children will be powerful in the land; his descendants will be blessed. His family will be wealthy and rich, and he will be prosperous forever. Psalm 112:1-3

Acknowledgements

I want to thank you, Lord Jesus, for Your most precious love for me and the blessing of being in your family. Thank You for the privilege I have to serve the lovely, precious girl You gave me, and our children and grandchildren You have entrusted to us, to disciple and then send out to change the world for Christ sake. Cover them, protect them and bring us all together one day with You and all that have gone before and those who will come after. Don't let us lose a single one.

I first want to acknowledge the incredible dedication and efforts of my precious family in writing this book. Rhonda has blessed me and believed in me when I didn't believe in myself. If I could attain a level of half her courage I know we could change the world. Our sweet children are our most incredible gift and our greatest prize. I am so proud of you, I can't stand it.

Thank you to David and Linda Smith for providing the example we needed in order to go away on our first family vision goal-setting weekend. Your lives and your family are a source of great encouragement to us.

The Greg Gunn Family
photo by Bethany Parkman

Thank you to Hannah, Hunter, Neveah, Bethany, Esther, Leah, Josiah, Moriah, and Jacob. I love you guys! I am the happiest daddy in the whole world.

To my wonderful parents Gordon and Bobbie Gunn, who taught me about Jesus, tucked me into bed at night, and sung me songs that I now sing to my kids to point them to God. You were truly laying the foundation for many Godly generations.

Thank you to my sister Robin, my brothers Philip and Nathan and their families, for being the encouragement I needed. You are truly my best friends; I wish everyone could meet you and know you like I do.

Each of you in our LifeGroup has provided us a sounding board we needed to develop the Family-iD workshop. Each of you will receive eternal rewards.

There are so many that I want to thank for their

contribution to this work, without them it would not have happened. First to those who believed in us and the Family Vision Ministry, when it was an infant, Mark and Kerri Naylor who helped us found the ministry in 1996, and David and Melissa Brown. Without your administration and curriculum development we would not be here today; you guys are my heroes.

Craig and Amy Groeschel, you guys have been our greatest encouragement since the day we met. Craig, your sermons have challenged me to hear the call of God on my life and step into that calling by faith. Thank you for leading us to walk by faith and not by sight. I am still mad at you for disrupting all my plans for our future. I thought I had it all planned out and you kept pointing out that our lives are not our own, but were bought with a price. Following the will of God is the only way to true fulfillment, happiness, and joy in this life and the life hereafter.

Our board of directors Joe and Shelly Gitthens, Eric and Marla Joiner, Travis and Kristi McCoy, Mark and Kerri Naylor and Rhonda Thomas. Each of you is a constant inspiration.

Our supporters who have given sacrificially over the years. You have no idea how precious you are to us; your gifts have blessed us and are going to bear fruit for generations to come. Scott and Laura Bowen, Mickey and Beverly Raney, Paul and Donna Iser, Eric and Marla Joiner, Brian and Marla Hill, Jantz and Michelle Kinzer, our Primerica Team, all of our Regional Vice Presidents, and many, many more. You guys have made this possible.

Those who helped with writing, editing and prayer, Randy, Sherri and Ashley Allsbury, thank you for taking the bull by the horns and literally single-handedly pushing this book over the finish line. I can't tell you how much I love and appreciate you. **Brannon Golden**, *you did some of the heaviest lifting and the countless hours will pay great dividends in the lives of families here and around the world.*

Family-iD Intentional Direction

Table of Contents

Foreword

As I'm typing this, I'm sitting on an airplane with my family traveling to California for our annual family vacation. To say that I'm excited is an understatement. Our crew has planned this get-away for quite some time. We saved our airline miles to purchase flights, reserved a Suburban big enough to haul all eight of us, rented a small house close to the beach, and have a host of activities lined up for sheer vacation bliss.

It's interesting to me what families plan for—and what they don't. Many of our friends might plan for a trip similar to ours. Others will plan to purchase a dining table, a car or a nicer home. Some even plan to help kids with a future college education. But most families I know don't have a well-thought-out plan to raise their children. Even the committed Christian families I know rarely think about how to help their children better know and serve Christ. You could say every family ends up somewhere; few end up somewhere on purpose.

That's why I'm excited by the fact that you are holding this book in your hand. Your family—those people that God has entrusted to your care—can end up somewhere on purpose—if you will begin with the end in mind.

That's what Greg Gunn told me the first time we had lunch together over a decade ago. What I thought would be just another lunch with a great guy from my church turned into a pivotal meeting for my life and family. With overwhelming passion, Greg barely touched his chicken sandwich as he vividly described to me all the plans he had for the Gunn family. "Our family is our most important ministry. And if we help them know Christ, we can change the world!" Greg blurted out with contagious faith.

By the end of our time together, I was intrigued. But as I observed the Gunn family in action over the years to come, I became convinced. Business and spiritual leaders aren't the only ones who should lead with vision and motivate others toward greatness. If any group in the world should be passionate about direction, vision, and values, it should be the Christ-centered family.

Even though most Christians I know would agree with Greg, most don't know where to start or what to do to train their children with godly principles. They have good intentions but don't know how to convert their intentions into actions. By default, they just coast along, hoping and praying for the best.

That's why I'm so thankful for The Family-iD. Greg's amazing book offers practical tools that will equip you to lead your family in a way that will create lasting memories and cultivate the hearts and minds of your children. You will have a vision for your family with a clear plan for spiritual and relational growth. You will learn to depend on each other for support instead of looking outside of your family for significance. If you prayerfully put these tools and principles into practice within your home, God will use you to lead your family to its exact and unique purpose.

When most families simply end up somewhere, yours can end up somewhere on purpose.

*---**Craig Groeschel**, Lifechurch.tv*

Introduction

Why is it so important to have a vision statement in writing and to discover your family's unique passion and purpose and then pass it on to your future generations? I believe it is a major part of God's plan for the redemption of all mankind. I am convinced that **"laying the foundations for many Godly generations"** is what God had in mind for every believer.

I want to thank you for the commitment you've made to your family in seeking God's Vision and Purpose for your family.

More often than not, it is not wrong motives, but wrong methods that keep families from fulfilling their dreams of love, harmony, and happiness.

I want to give you hope through the process of developing your own family purpose. In my life, this has been the most exciting adventure I have ever experienced. I feel that I am fulfilling a destiny as the leader of my family. No longer am I going to let life just happen, sweeping us along with the flow of society's values and trends, without any sense of a purpose, a map, a compass, or an overall guiding plan. All of nature has a purpose. It is the DNA and the chromosomal structure of every cell. This purpose tells every cell what it is and how it functions. It tells the cell what it will become and how it relates to every other cell.

Let me try to sum up what I am saying. Your Family-ID is the single most important decision your family will ever make! Why? Because it will govern every decision you will ever make.

– Greg Gunn

Family-iD --- Intentional Direction

Preface

I know a thing or two about kids. My wife Rhonda and I have seven of them. They're all boys—except five of them. When we had our seventh child, Rhonda and I figured we were about half done. But then my oldest daughter got married, and they have (so far) brought us one grandchild, so that raised the competitive stakes yet again. But Rhonda and I have a head start, and I aim for us to keep it.

Somebody asked me recently, "Greg, have you ever considered what might be causing all these children?"

I answered, "Well, we have it narrowed down to two things. And if it's the one I *think* it is, we're not stopping now." (He left me alone after that.)

The Past Is Past

As you begin to think about how you can develop your family's vision, maybe you're concerned about your past mistakes. You have the best intentions to build up a great family, but you fear that the patterns and the consequences of your old missteps are going to come back to haunt you, to sabotage your ability to pull this off. That's simply not so.

What God wants to do in your life is lay a foundation for many Godly generations. Maybe you think you've heard all this before. And maybe it made you feel like you were just hearing all the thousands of ways you'd already been messing it up. I prefer a different approach. The future is where God is calling us. There's no sense spending any more time in the past. Don't feel condemned for things that can't be undone. I can't give you something I don't have, and one thing I don't have, is condemnation for you. You can't change the past anyway. Instead, focus on the future. *Your* future. By doing so, we can all work together to raise a higher standard for families. For *your* family.

Since Mark Naylor and I first began leading weekend Family Vision Workshops, we haven't yet encountered a family who had the wrong motives for attending. No one's ever said to me, "Greg, my goal is to have an absolutely horrible marriage, to have rebellious kids, and to one day see them all strung out on drugs." Nobody ever plans for those things. They do happen, but I'd argue it's in the *absence* of a plan.

The truth is, people *can* envision the wonderful results they want to achieve. Most often, however, they simply don't know the correct methods to get them there. They don't know *how* to build their household into an awesome, joyful family whose solid values span across generations. The fact that you're taking the initiative to craft a vision for your family proves it: you're looking for what God has for them and for you. So let me encourage you: Hebrews 11:6 tells us that God rewards those who diligently seek Him. God will give you what you're looking for. Keep going!

The Foundation of Ideas

In 1996, Rhonda and I were visiting with David and Linda Smith at the church we attended. I was teasing David a little, asking him where he had been the weekend before. He answered, "Well, actually...my wife and I went on our annual family goal-setting weekend. Once a year, my wife and I go somewhere alone, and we spend about two and a half days working on writing goals for each family member, goals for each other, and goals for our marriage. We pray together and ask God to reveal to us what his plan is for our family and for our future generations."

At that time, Rhonda and I had been married for twelve years, and honestly, that thought had never crossed my mind. I might have considered doing something like that for my business, but never for my family! I was intrigued, and I asked him if he would be willing to write out an agenda of what they did on that weekend. He graciously agreed, and Rhonda and I went away for a three-day weekend of our own, agenda in hand, and we tried it. We still have the original piece of paper, written in pencil.

During our time away, we prayed and asked God what he wants our family to accomplish on this earth. We asked not just in this generation, but for the generations to come. We prayed specifically over what the Bible says in Jeremiah 35, about the power of generational thinking. We asked God to bless our family with a unique vision, one that would capture the hearts and imaginations of our children. And not just for this generation— not just our immediate children—but one that would capture children we may never even meet.

That weekend, when we first began writing, God began to speak out of the end of my pen. If that sounds strange to you, consider this: there are 66 books of the Bible that prove that God speaks out of the end of a pen. As you begin to write your own family vision, we sincerely believe God will reveal Himself to you through your pen. We want you to arrive at the other end of this process with your family vision, your family mission statement, and a list of your core family values, all in writing.

When Rhonda and I came back from our weekend away, we were on fire. We returned to the small Bible study group we led in our home, and we shared with them what we had experienced. We were so excited! I kept talking about it every week. After about six months, I asked, "So…How many of you have taken some time away together to write your family vision?" One couple raised their hands.

One couple?

It just seemed so hard for people to follow through. What was I going to have to do to convince my friends how life-changing this process could be? I was so frustrated, I considered lighting myself on fire. (Fortunately for all of us, I came up with a much better, more practical, longer-term solution.) We packed up everybody in our group, took them off to a retreat center, and stayed there until everybody had cranked out a family vision statement.

And that was the beginning of the Family Vision Weekend. Since 1997, more than two thousand families have been through Family iD Workshops, from all over the United States and Canada. That first couple, the only ones to raise their hands, Mark and Kerri Naylor, have partnered together with Rhonda and me to conduct this ministry ever since.

Thinking Generationally

The Gunn family vision statement is "Laying the foundation for many Godly generations." We deliberately made our vision statement one that we will not be able to accomplish in our lifetimes. We want our future generations to still be working toward accomplishing that same goal.

A vision is important. It's compelling, a powerful driver in our lives. According to the Bible, "Where there is no vision (no redemptive revelation of God), the people perish (throw off restraint)." In that verse, Proverbs 29:18, the Hebrew word for "perish" is the same one used in Exodus 32:25. In Exodus, Moses had just returned from Mount Sinai with the Ten Commandments, only to find the Israelites dancing around "naked," "without restraint," "out of control," worshiping the golden calf that Aaron had made to appease them.

We live in a culture today that seems to me to have cast off restraint. It's lost its bearings, its moral compass as a civilization. God is calling people like us—a Gideon's army, a small contingent, as recorded in Judges 7—to show the world that having a family vision, a family mission, and a core set of family values is a meaningful way to demonstrate that where there's a lot of sin, it just means there's a lot more room for grace.

I grew up going to church. My mom and dad were Christians. My grandparents were Christians. My folks took me to church every time the doors were open. In Ada, Oklahoma, the little town where I grew up, there were about 150 people in our entire congregation. Our youth group consisted of about 40 teenagers. There were 25 or so core families in the church. I remember looking back once and trying to count the number of people from my old church who are today serving God in a more powerful way than their parents did. How many would you guess? I could count maybe five of those 40 who are more on fire for God today than their parents were. In my opinion, that's a terrible return on investment. Children who grow up in a Christian home ought to emerge from that household, at the very least, *liking* God. That seems like a pretty simple, worthwhile goal.

Cookie Dough

Every family is like a batch of cookie dough. Every family puts together its own batch of cookie dough—the kids—and each family has its own specific recipe. Some families have more sugar than other families do. Some put candy in theirs. Some have a few nuts. (You know which ones I'm talking about.) Each family wads up the cookie dough and places it on a cookie sheet, and then they slide it into the oven. The oven is the teenage years.

The parents stand around the oven and say things like, "I wonder how mine are going to turn out?" and, "I sure hope mine turn out well."

Another couple might offer, "I think yours are going to turn out great. You guys seem to have a great family."

Then at age 21, they open the oven and pull out the cookie sheet. Now they say things like, "Oh, look! Two out of three of ours turned out really good. One of them got a little burned around the edges." Another couple stands over theirs, crying, because all four of theirs turned out terrible. In fact, one of theirs fell off the cookie sheet onto a heating element and burned to a crisp.

Another couple beams. All of theirs turned out wonderful: they became doctors, lawyers, astronauts, and missionaries. When other people ask them, "How did yours turn out so well?" they say, "We don't really know. We just give God all the glory. He must have done it." And if you ask the couple whose kids didn't turn out, "What happened?" they say, "We don't know. We did the best we knew how to do."

When Rhonda and I began thinking seriously about our kids and their future, we recognized that a daunting task lay before us: "There has to be something we can do that can cause our kids to want to serve God more powerfully than we have served Him. We have to lay some foundation." When we would try to talk to other people about it, more often than not, what we heard back were things like, "Greg, you just kind of have to cross your fingers and hope that they turn out. In fact, you can actually do everything right, and it's really just the luck of the draw."

Needless to say, that did not encourage us.

PART ONE: STIR IT UP

Chapter 1: Why a Vision?

In the little church where I grew up, I believed that if the parents were warm for God, then the children who grew up in that family would be hot. And then their children, having grown up in a hot household, would be *nuclear!* But in fact, in a lot of cases the opposite seems to be true. The tendency is that if Mom and Dad are warm, then their children are just cool, the next generation is cold, and the next generation is frozen.

At the Christian university I attended, there was this saying around campus: "Show me a preacher's kid, and I'll show you a mess. Show me a missionary's kid, and I'll show you a *real* mess." Of course that's a horrible generalization. I'd like to believe it's not true in most cases. But, it was true enough that it was a running joke among the students. It just doesn't seem to make sense: If you're the child of a missionary, you're basically growing up in a 365-day discipleship program in the field. How could someone possibly come out of that and not even like God?

The Great Disconnect

I believe a gigantic disconnect exists in our minds, really just a mirage-like separation between worlds, the spiritual and the secular. Consider a successful businessperson. I own my own business, and my partner in ministry, Mark, also owns a business. Certain basic principles are required to run a successful business. You have to have a decent business plan. You have to have goals. You try to leave as little as possible to chance. You try to maximize your efficiency by making sure everything you do has a purpose, and furthermore that that purpose serves the business. You want everyone in the organization to know exactly what you're doing. Yet the same successful businessperson goes home, and he doesn't have a clue. It's as though he thinks everything that he wants to happen at home is just going to happen by accident—that somehow it's just going to come together.

Think about a successful football coach. To get the most out of his team, he has to have a personal relationship with every one of his players. In my own experience, by getting a hold on my heart, my coach got me to accomplish things that before I didn't even know I *could* do. Yet the same coach, the one who knows exactly what it takes to build a great team, to get the most out of those players, goes home, and he doesn't have a clue. He doesn't understand how to build a relationship with his own child.

Now think about a successful pastor. He builds a great church, a ministry organization that reaches masses of people. Billy Graham knows that in order to have a successful crusade, he has to send people in two years before he gets there, a prayer team to begin "softening up the ground." Then he has to send in a group of trainers to teach lay people how to minister to and pray for the many who will come down to the front during the crusade. Every successful ministry has to have a plan. And yet, so often we see that same successful pastor doesn't know how to connect with his own family.

The "Coach Effect"

God wants to restore a connection in all of our lives. But how can we bring it about? How do we accomplish all that God wants us to accomplish with our lives? The answer is actually based in a deceptively simple principle: The coach has a significant bearing on the outcome of the game. According to a June 24, 2009, article in *USA Today*, Bob Stoops, the head football coach at the University of Oklahoma, will receive "more than $30 million through the end of 2015." Part of that is $3.675 million for the 2009-2010 season, with an annual "stay" bonus of $700,000. The University of Oklahoma seems to be convinced that Bob Stoops has some influence on how the games turn out. God has given us the same opportunity to be the coach in our families. God wants us to set the agenda, to write the plays, to call the plays, and to lead our families to victory.

The Purpose of a Vision

Remember, Proverbs 29:18 says, "Where there is no

vision, the people perish." According to this verse, you have to have a vision to even survive. That seems like an extreme statement to make, so let's explore what it could mean.

Your family vision will serve you as a compass. You most need a compass when there are no landmarks in sight, or when it's absolutely dark. But your family vision doesn't only serve you; it will act as a compass for your future generations as well. They'll be able to look to that family vision and find direction for what God has called them to do. The vision God gives to you will resonate inside their very DNA.

Your family vision will also act as a rudder. A rudder is the paddle-shaped control that typically hangs underneath a ship, near the rear of the hull. It controls the direction of the ship. In comparison with the rest of a ship, the rudder is very small. And yet it sets the course for the entire ship. No matter how the wind is blowing, your family vision statement will become a rudder for the children's, children's children in your family.

Your family vision will also act as a telescope. Your family will be able to look off into the distant future through that telescope and see what you envisioned for them. Future generations will look into your telescope, and they'll be able to see the mental picture that God gave you, for what He has called them to accomplish.

Ed Cole, a great men's minister, once said, "Without a vision, we will always return to our past." When I was a kid, in church, when someone "returned to their past," we had a word for that: *Backsliding.* It meant that someone had abandoned their faith in Christ and returned to a life of sin, separated from God. They had "slid back" to where they were before. Even worse, it carries the connotation that any ground a person may have gained in their lifetime has now been lost. God does not call us to relive our past. God calls us to a future. God is calling us to do something powerful with our lives.

The Power of a Vision

In business, I've heard a saying: "Show me a third-generation company, and I'll show you a company that's going out of business." Now, if it's a family business, you'd think that a boy or girl would grow up working for the business, dad would teach them the ropes, and then one great day, with much pomp, in a purposeful rite of passage, the father would pass the business on to the child. But that rarely happens.

Here's why: a company doesn't actually begin as a company. It begins as an idea, a vision, really just a glimmer of hope for a future yet to be realized. The original founder of the company—whether it was Grandpa, Great Grandpa, or Great, Great, Great, Great Grandpa—one day had a fire in his belly. When he couldn't shake that fire, he committed his ideas to paper. Then gradually, likely over the course of many years, using that blueprint as his guide, he built a company around that vision.

Let's say that man does teach his daughter the basic tenets of the business: "Here's how you land a client, here's how you write a contract," and so on. She really gets it, and she manages things well. Gradually he gives her more and more responsibility, and then when he feels she's ready, he retires and hands everything over to her.

The truth is, most of us can hand down the assets, even the processes, but not the vision. A business can actually run on autopilot for a while—perhaps many years—still appearing successful to the casual observer. But then one day, the business finds itself in the hands of a grandson, who's so far away from the his grandfather's original vision that, just as soon as he inherits the assets and the business, he drives it right into the ground.

It wasn't the nuts and bolts, the systems, that built the business. The critical component which built the assets was not knowledge, nor was it even people. It was the vision. It was the passion inspired by the vision.

Vision Creates Passion

Although a vision is an intangible element, the reason it's so powerful and so critical to long-term success is that it generates passion. If a person has no passion, it doesn't mean they have a passion problem. It means they have a vision problem. Vision creates passion.

Tiger Woods has passion for the game of golf. That's most

likely because he's had a vision for golf since he was a very small child. There's a story that when Tiger Woods was a kid, he tacked Jack Nicklaus' winning tournament record on the headboard of his bead. Every night before he went to bed, he'd look at it. It reminded him of what he wanted right before he'd turn off the lights to go to sleep. Then, as soon as he awoke the next morning, it was right there, waiting to remind him again. Tiger Woods had a vision. And that vision created a passion in him.

Most Bible scholars agree that David wrote most of the Psalms. The contents of the Psalms reveal the inner life of a complicated man with passionate feelings, spanning the course of a lifetime. David had something special helping him sustain that level of passion throughout his entire life. Psalm 78:2-4 says, "I will open my mouth in parables, I will utter hidden things, things from of old—what we have heard and known, what our fathers have told us. We will not hide them from their children; we will tell the next generation the praiseworthy deeds of the Lord, his power, and the wonders he has done." David spent all of his reflective time, as a shepherd looking over his flocks, rehearsing, recounting, contemplating—even singing—all the praiseworthy deeds of his God. Constantly gazing on the mental picture of what God had done in the past for the people of Israel. This gave David a clear understanding of God's nature. And as this passage says, it was important to him to share that passion with his children. Vision creates passion.

Passion Lives for Others

People who possess great passion rarely live for themselves. Most see themselves as a part of something greater, a great cloud of witnesses making up the fabric that serves the larger vision. This kind of perspective equips them for selflessness.

In the church where I was raised, we spent what I'd consider an unhealthy amount of time focused on "eschatology." (Eschatology is the study of the end times, from a Biblical perspective.) In that environment, I basically determined that I was not going to be old enough to have children before the Lord came back. I *always* thought the Lord would be coming back sometime in the next five years. If you're reading this, then most likely means it hasn't happened yet. So inevitably, His return has to be sometime in the *next* five. Maybe that seems odd to you, but consider this: there were those in the New Testament who believed He would be coming back in their lifetimes. I believe now that this mindset was largely a distraction our enemy (Satan) had sent, causing me to lack a vision for myself beyond the next five years.

Now let me just say clearly: the Lord *is* coming back. He promised, therefore He will. But...what if He tarries yet another 500 years?

I read once about a Japanese automobile company that wrote a 200-year business plan for their company. If my manager assigned me to that committee, I'd slap him! We're willing to put that much time and effort into writing a plan for nothing but the love of money. Perhaps we should consider doing the same for the love of God in our lives. If you were to write a 200-year plan for your family, what would it look like?

Plymouth Rock

I love history. I've studied the lives of the Pilgrims in depth. One hundred and two Pilgrims boarded the Mayflower. They floated across the ocean for 66 days. They were more or less packed together in the hull of that ship. No bathroom. No shower. The trip that brought them to Plymouth took over two months. *Two months!* That's tremendous commitment, not to mention colossal risk. And it was all because of a vision they had, a vision for a better life.

And once they got there, it's not like they came down the gangplank, strolling off the ship, waving to a cheering crowd, streamers and confetti everywhere, straight into the Holiday Inn Express for a nice, hot shower. Even following a trip like that, it didn't get much easier. It's not like they came over to retire. The average person in those times lived to about 45 years old. They didn't come over here to pick up their green union card and receive their standard two-week paid vacation.

According to a book I read years ago, one hundred and

two people landed at Plymouth Rock. During that first winter, 52 of them died of starvation or sickness. Many watched their families dwindle away, one family member passing after another. And of the 50 survivors at the end of the winter, none of them said, "Forget this! I'm going back to England! I can't stand this. You've got to be kidding! I didn't come over here to watch each one of my kids die. I'm going back." None hopped a boat and headed back. Not one.

They weren't living for themselves. They were thinking about the generations who would follow them. They were thinking about their children, but even more than that, they were thinking about their children's children, and about their children's, children's children. If they could stick it out, the lives of those who would follow them would be exponentially better than anything any of them had experienced for themselves. Those Pilgrims had a vision. And that vision created a passion. Passion like that gives a person immense power. Today the descendants of those people are called The Mayflower Society and they have grown to 33 million people. Wow!

The Declaration of Independence

Fifty-six men signed the Declaration of Independence; some of them had descended from the original 50 Pilgrims. Just imagine being one of those 56, representing the thirteen colonies on that hot July day in Philadelphia: "We mutually pledge to each other our lives, our fortunes and our sacred honor to defend and protect these states." Of those 56 men, few survived for long. Several lost sons, and most would themselves end up shot and killed. Nine of them died during the war, either from its hardships or its bullets. Understand: These men were not wild-eyed pirates. They were not homeless. They were the most respected men in their communities. They were business owners and leaders, pillars of their contemporary society.

Although freedom is priceless, it can only be purchased at great cost. Think about the significance of that seemingly simple, six-second task of signing that document. It was treason against the crown. It was signing your own death warrant. Upon learning of the existence of the Declaration, of course, the first people the

British leadership would target would be its signatories. John Hancock pushed the envelope for courage. According to popular legend, Hancock deliberately signed in such large script "that King George could read it without his spectacles." Whether that's true or not, there's no arguing that his signature dwarfs most of the others. By an act of his will, he chose to challenge an unjust king.

Now, just imagine it was you who had the opportunity to sign that document. When you got home from Philadelphia, how would you explain it to your wife, to your family? I can just imagine my conversation with Rhonda:

RHONDA: "You did *what?* You signed our name to *what?* Have you lost your mind? Do you realize when the British find out, they're going to come tromping over here, and they're going kill all of us—first thing? They're going to burn our house down! We just got this house paid off! What were you *thinking?*"

ME: "But Honey, everybody was signing it. I didn't want to be the odd man out!"

What drove them, what motivated them, was their extraordinary vision? Consider how unlikely that vision even was.

All the odds were against them. It would be almost impossible for them to win. There would be no support from a mother country. In fact, that "mother country" was going to do everything in her power to utterly destroy them! There would be no "home" to return to if things didn't work out, whether in the colonies or overseas.

And even if they *did* win, then the real hardship would begin. "Congratulations! You've just won your own country! Now you have to form a government, provide for essential services, and negotiate favorable terms with other established countries who, by the way, are hesitant to even acknowledge you as an ongoing concern—let alone as a sovereign nation."

It was the power of vision that drove them. Vision creates passion.

Other Visionary Heroes

Patrick Henry stood up before the Continental Congress and questioned his peers. Is it worth it to go to war against England? That depends. Can England tell Americans how we should worship? Can England dictate to Americans where we can live? "Is life so dear? Is peace so sweet as to be purchased with chains and slavery? God forbid. But as for me, give me liberty or give me death." The power of vision compelled Patrick Henry. His vision was for freedom, liberty.

What is it that you want from this life? Is your vision worth dying for? Vision creates that kind of passion.

Nathan Hale was a schoolteacher. He was dispatched into enemy territory to spy on the British. Unfortunately, upon his return crossing enemy lines, he was captured by them. He was prepared for hanging in the commons, with a noose placed around his neck and tightened. He was provided the opportunity for last words. He began, "I have but one regret..." Just imagine all of the things he might have regretted. Leaving his wife without her husband, his children without their father. Leaving the land that his parents had purchased with their blood, their sweat, their tears. He said, "I have but one regret: that I have but one life to give for my country." He was willing to give his life for his vision, again and again. Vision creates passion.

John Paul Jones was the commander of the American Navy—all four of her ships. In fact, one of them was a canoe with a cannon placed in the front of it. Imagine facing off against literally the most powerful navy on earth under those circumstances. When they exchanged fire, the British pounded Jones' ship so full of holes that his mast fell. With no mast, even the finest ship is quite literally dead in the water. Dead and dying sailors lay all around him, his boat in flames. Lighting his last match, preparing to light his last cannon, the British officers called out to him from across the water, "Mr. Jones, have you had enough?" He called back, "I have not yet begun to fight!"

A man or a woman with vision in possession of passion is afforded great power, power to totally commit. A person with passion is able to ignore his own hurt, his own suffering. Vision creates that kind of passion.

I want to cast a vision so powerful that it captures the hearts of my children. The world spends literally billions of dollars every year trying to capture my kids' hearts and imaginations. And the world has the money to see it through. All I have, the only thing I can possibly use to compete, is my vision. My vision will fuel me with passion, which will be contagious in my family. And that passion will absolutely change their lives.

Passion Creates Discipline

Have you ever known someone who seems to have zero discipline? What causes that? Let me assure you: they don't have a discipline problem. What they have is a passion problem. Psalm 78:7 says, "That they might set their hope in God and not forget the works of God, but might keep His commandments." According to this verse, the cause-effect relationship of setting your hope in God is that, ultimately, it will help you keep his commandments. Passion creates discipline.

Harriet Tubman

Harriet Tubman is a great example of passion. Born and raised in Maryland as a slave, she was frequently hired out by her owners to work at various plantations. As an adult, Tubman managed to escape to Philadelphia in the North. But even after she had made it, she soon felt God calling her to return to the South to free others. Over time, she made thirteen trips back, freeing more than seventy slaves, taking advantage of the network we know today as the Underground Railroad.

At the time of her rescues, slave owners in the South never suspected it was a former slave who was helping all those people escape, let alone a woman. They said this mysterious leader was invisible. Among the abolitionist and the slaves, she earned the nickname "Moses," because of her determination and success in setting her people free. If Harriet Tubman had been living for herself, she would not have made thirteen trips back. She would have made precisely one: her own.

Passion creates discipline. Passion gives you the power to totally commit and totally sell out.

Pilgrim Mama

Let's talk again about the Pilgrims for a moment. Consider the reality of their everyday lives. What a powerful price they paid, simply trying to clear just one acre at a time. Their hope was to grow enough crops to survive, and for what? So they could clear more land, so they could grow more crops. For those who first came, it was a race against time, to accomplish as much productive physical labor as they could before they died. In the end, their vision was to pass on the fruits of all that labor to the generation who would immediately follow them.

Now consider this scenario: a Pilgrim papa comes in from the fields. His wife has their eight kids gathered there around the table, and he says, "You know, I'm just not happy. I've decided I'm going to leave. I do love you guys, but I really just need to find myself. We only get one time around in this life, and I'm convinced that God wants me to be happy."

I don't really have to stretch much to imagine what that Pilgrim mama would do. She'd grab that man by the collar, slap him a few times and say, "Listen, buddy! We didn't come over here to get happy! We came over here to lay a foundation. And if we *happen* to get happy in the process, big guy, that's just icing on the cake. Now, you get out there and shoot us some dinner, because we're hungry!" Pilgrim papa would pull himself together, pick up his gun, and scoot outside to look for some turkey, deer, rabbit, or squirrel.

That whole scene seems just silly to us now. Or does it?

A few years ago, a friend of mine walked into my office and said, "Greg, I think I'm going to leave my family. I think I'm done. I'm just not happy. I feel like I owe it to myself to go out and find some happiness." Because of the culture we live in, a culture of plenty, it can be easy for you and me to fall right in with someone in a situation like his. To a certain extent, maybe we can sympathize, at least emotionally. I believe it's because we've placed so much emphasis on comfort, on making ourselves happy in this present moment, that we fail to build anything of lasting value.

Whatever happened to making a commitment and keeping it? We should do what we say we're going to do. People are depending on us. Zig Ziglar used to say that if you would help enough other people get what they want, then they would help you get what you want. Put the focus on others, rather than on yourself. That's a very powerful principle. It's just as effective inside your family as it is outside, in other relationships.

Discipline Creates Total Commitment

I believe God is calling us to change the world. He wants us to become men and women of vision. Discipline and commitment go hand in hand. When you begin to put into practice the tiny daily steps that are required to move you toward fulfilling your ultimate vision, over time, you become completely invested. When a person has established regular, effective discipline, hiccups in their progress barely affect them, because they are totally sold out. They know where they're going.

Examples and Promises

Dr. Martin Luther King had vision. He spoke those four little words, "I have a dream..." in 1963. More than 45 years later, they still echo in our ears. I believe they will continue to resonate for generations, for hundreds and hundreds of years. His vision was so powerful, and his discipline to speak the truth was so complete, that he passed that vision on to us, people far beyond even his own family! "I have a dream that one day this nation will rise up and live out the true meaning of its creed: 'We hold these truths to be self-evident, that all men are created equal'... I have a dream that my four little children will one day live in a nation where they will not be judged by the color of their skin, but by the content of their character." What a dream. What a vision. Ultimately, of course, that dream would cost him (and us) his life. He paid the ultimate price.

Psalm 78:7 says, "Then they would put their trust in God and would not forget his deeds but would keep his commands." It's our responsibility to pass on the truth we know to our children and then to our children's children. To me, that's what this scripture is about. It's telling us that if we can help our children trust in God, and if we can pass on to them the stories of what he's done, that they will respond by honoring him (keeping his commands). Certainly we who are parents must pass this truth on to our children.

Grandparents have an even greater opportunity, and as a result perhaps even more responsibility. A grandparent has more influence in their little finger than a parent has in their entire body. You will have unique opportunities to share vision in quiet moments with the added bonus that happy memories will be attached. The picture that you can paint in the heart of your grandchild will impact the generations which will follow them— *your* legacy.

Of course the ultimate example of all of these principles is Christ:

Jesus had a vision (imputed to him by his father, not insignificantly) to reconcile humanity to God. His vision was bigger than himself and could only be accomplished with God's involvement and that vision created passion within him. Jesus spoke to literally thousands of people at a time, and his influence changed their lives and the course of history.

Passion puts others first. In almost every instance where Jesus performed some miracle in the Gospels, he was actually on his way somewhere else. When he cast the legion of demons out of the possessed man, when the woman with the issue of blood touched his hem and was healed, when he spoke the word and healed the Roman centurion's servant—on each of these occasions, he was actually on his way somewhere else, and he allowed his own pressing travels to be "interrupted" with the thing that was most important to each of those individuals.

Passion gives you the power to become disciplined. Jesus hand-picked a team of individuals for what purpose? To *disciple* them, methodically pouring into them in such a way that each would ultimately give their lives for the vision he had placed inside them: that Jesus was the Messiah, and that accepting his coming would redeem all who received him.

Discipline yields the strength to totally commit. With the foundation for the Church laid, Jesus endured unsubstantiated accusations, unlawful treatment, beating and torture, and finally his own death, even death on a cross. "Yet not *my* will, Father, but yours." He was committed to the outcome of his vision, no matter what it cost him personally.

Your Future Is Not the Past

Let's look at Psalm 78:7 again, this time in a different version (NLT), and let's take it even further, through verse 8: "So each generation should set its hope anew on God, not forgetting his glorious miracles and obeying his commands. Then they will not be like their ancestors—stubborn, rebellious, and unfaithful, refusing to give their hearts to God."

There's a really funny scene in the Will Smith movie *Hitch,* where Hitch takes the young woman Sara, whom he's trying to win over, to Ellis Island to reconnect her with her ancestry. In a poignant moment, she sees her great-great-grandfather Juan's name in the rolls, and she runs from the room, crying. Once she's able to regain her composure, she explains that her family has spent generations trying to escape the horrible legacy he left them. Hitch apologizes, "I'm really sorry. When I saw him on the computer and it said, 'The Butcher of Cadíz,' I thought it was a profession...not a headline."

Maybe you've struggled with mistakes and poor choices in your own life, or if you've looked back into your family history and thought, *it's no wonder I haven't been successful. Just look at the sorry stock I've come from!* If so, then the promise contained in Psalm 78:7-8 should give you hope. You can be that generation that "sets its hope *anew* on God." If you remember his miracles, you can obey his commands. And if you can do that, you won't be like your ancestors. Your family tree can change—starting with you. And you can pass that legacy on to your children, turning them hot, perhaps even nuclear.

You Have What It Takes

Don't fall for the lie that "You don't have it in you" to overcome, to make that change in your generation. Just 150 short years after the Pilgrims landed in this country, their descendants would stand against their greatest challenge yet: facing off against the mightiest military force on the planet, the British army. As George Washington desperately canvassed the countryside to raise an army, it wasn't West Point graduates he was recruiting. Perhaps you'll see parallels in these men to another famous story from history: they were fishermen, accountants, doctors, farmers. They weren't brilliant military minds and trained Navy Seals. They were ordinary men.

British invasion was inevitable, indeed, imminent. Washington would ride into a town, enter the church, ring the steeple bell, and wait. People would pour in from the fields to find out what was going on. Then this imposing figure of a man, more than six feet tall, would stand up before the group and make his impassioned pitch. He would explain that the British were coming. That they were going to burn the very church in which they were standing. That they would take the land by force. That everything that these men and women had worked so hard for, died for, they and their parents, and their parents' parents, was all going to come to nothing. King George III was demanding his due, and he didn't care to hear what his subjects had to say about it. And George Washington would ask, "Who among you is willing to fight?"

I can imagine many of the responses. I can picture a farmer saying, "For two summers, the crops didn't come in. During each of the winters that followed, I became a marksman with my squirrel gun. I can hit a squirrel on the run from 100 yards, a dead shot to the head, so I don't waste any of the meat. I can certainly hit a British soldier from 1,000 yards." And of course, it only helped his odds that the British would be banging drums, wearing bright red coats with white pants!

Of course, they had a choice. They didn't have to fight. They could have just accepted their fate, let the chips fall where they may, and lived with the outcome, however it resolved itself. They could have carried on with their lives as always, loyal subjects to the crown, essentially as slaves and sharecroppers. That could have been the inheritance they would leave to their children. The legacy they would leave...to us. Of course, we know what they chose. We know the pain they endured, the commitment, and the loss. And we know the ultimate outcome of their sacrifice as well, a sacrifice they were willing to make because they had a vision for the future. The future they envisioned is our present, the freedoms we enjoy today, more than 200 years later.

Well, guess what? We're in a fight today, too. Make no mistake. There's a war on to bring about the demise of our families, to take them out. Just look around you. Money is no object to the industry of self-destruction. Forgive me for saying it, but our culture has made most of us into a bunch of pansies, unwilling to make sacrifices for the things we claim that we believe. So once again in our history, we stand in the valley of decision. We can go with the flow and just accept the inevitable outcome of the slow-motion train wreck that goes along with the erosion of values and morality. Or we can choose to stand. We can choose to pay the price for victory. We can make ourselves worthy to stand beside the thousands of other families who have already chosen, already drawn their line in the sand.

We may look silly at first. We certainly won't look like everybody else. We won't dress the same way they do. We won't consume the same kinds of entertainment that they do. We won't cast off restraint in our lifestyles, and we won't accept such low standards for our own children. But we will overflow with love in our families. Our families will not live for themselves, but for others. We will build a healthy, sustainable culture within our households, where not only are our children protected and comforted, but where they are proud to contribute, excited to share their passion.

Your future begins today. Your children's future begins today. Your grandchildren's future begins today. The future of children you will never see is in your hands. You are their ancestor. What will your legacy be? You can begin to build a life today that will stand. The past is past. You can change today. And by changing today—each day, one day at a time—you can literally change the course of the future. You can lay the foundation for many future generations.

God is calling you. He is calling us. "Who among you is willing to fight?" What about you? Are you ready to fight?

Greg C. Gunn

Chapter 2: Establish Your Foundation

(I asked my ministry partner Mark Naylor to write this chapter.)

My wife Kerri and I have six children, ranging in age from 6 to 20. I can tell you all their names, but I can't begin to tell you their exact ages. It's not my fault—every year they keep changing them. What is it about women? Every time a woman learns I have six children, she always asks, "Oh, what are their ages?" Men never ask anything like that. I used to struggle and try to remember, and then finally, one time a couple of years ago I simply answered, "I have no idea." The woman asking looked stunned, like she'd just been frozen in time. But she didn't ask me anything else after that, so I thought, "This works." I've done it ever since.

Our experience after years of leading Family Vision Workshops is that the majority of people who express an interest in developing a "Family Vision"…actually have families. (That likely comes as no surprise.) But what this means to you in practical terms is that our primary audience tends to be couples— husbands and wives who are married to each other. Most feel that they could do a better job as spouses and parents, so they're eager to hear whatever ideas we can offer them. Many have already been doing a great job, and they just want to expand their options for success. Others are trying to overcome past hurdles and mistakes in their relationships, and they're looking for new beginnings on a firm foundation. We also frequently teach couples who are engaged to be married, just about to begin their new lives together. For these reasons, we want to be completely forthcoming; telling you honestly that much of what we discuss will come across as though it's directed mostly at couples and families.

However, in recent years, we've been observing a growing, exciting trend. Many of the people coming to our workshops are younger and younger, and many of them are single. As this new generation of Christ-followers diligently seeks all that He is, and all that He has for them, they're eager to avoid mistakes and find the narrow path. They want to be the best husbands and wives they can for the spouses they're trusting God to bring into their lives. It's really amazing. Just imagine if, the first time you met a potential new mate, you discovered that they'd already been preparing themselves to love you and your children, for generations to come. If you're single, please just understand where we're coming from. We're really glad to have you. You won't be sorry. When we talk in terms of couples and spouses, please just consider the communication options that we're addressing as being directly between you and Christ. You're awesome. God will honor your diligence more than you can possibly imagine.

We're going to look now at the basic concepts you'll need to understand before you set about the business of actually writing your family's Mission Statement. You might be tempted to just scan through this part, not really digging into it in depth. Don't do that. Stick with us.

Right now, find a special, blank piece of paper—preferably a color other than white. Don't succumb to the temptation to simply use a plain white sheet, or some random sheet out of a spiral notebook you just happen to have lying around. If you do, it will just disappear into a pile somewhere later, probably never to surface again. (You *know* it's true.) If you use a special color, you'll actually be able to find it later when you need it. As soon as you have it, write "The Father's Blueprint" across the top in big letters. (When Greg and I lead our Family iD Workshops, we actually have a blue sheet in our workbook that's already labeled like this for you.)

As you're going through all the material we're going to present to you, certain things will jump out more than others. Your special paper is where you'll capture that. Whenever it happens, write down, in your own words, two things:

1. What it was that caught your attention? Directly next to that,
2. What you think God would want you to do about that? In both

cases, please be as specific as possible.

Right Beginnings

Let's go ahead and get this out of the way: Satan hates your family. It's true. The Bible says in John 10:10 that "The thief (Satan) comes only to *steal* and *kill* and *destroy*." (Emphasis mine.) He hates your family because God ordained it. If you can fulfill God's purpose for your family, you represent a direct threat to his kingdom. Jesus commissioned us to make disciples using the time we have in this life. Discipleship is the transfer of wisdom and meaning over time, facilitated through intimate relationship. No better institution exists to foster true discipleship than family. So Satan wants you out of the way.

If the enemy can keep discipleship from happening within your family, then he can cause God's wisdom to skip generations. Consider his principal strategy throughout most of the Old Testament: good king, bad king. Bad king, good king. Every time he was able to skip a generation, God's people essentially had to start over. They were never able to get any traction toward fulfilling God's will for their nation. It ultimately took Jesus assuming his rightful place as the King of kings to break that cycle.

If it's true that Satan hates your family (and it clearly is), then the most obvious relationship he's likely to attack is between the husband and wife. Because they're at the center of the family unit, if their relationship is in jeopardy, it places the entire family at risk. For this reason, couples—and in fact, the entire family—must make their relationship the highest priority in the family.

We all know families who exist primarily for their children. Whether the entire family is centered around the baby's sleeping schedule or the kids' dance practice and soccer games, focusing on relationships other than between husband and wife dilutes the effectiveness of their opportunities for discipleship relationships. When couples get together, most often it's because they find they have shared interests, values, and goals. Certainly children are frequently one of those. But then, when the children do come, because they require so much time and attention, we can get sidetracked from what made us effective in the first place. The greatest benefit children can receive from your family is to learn how to have healthy, fulfilled relationships, and to learn firsthand what it means to serve Christ through their lives. They learn those things from watching you.

Making the marriage relationship the priority relationship in the family requires commitment. Many of us are *involved* in our family relationships, but we're not particularly *committed*. It may be hard to distinguish between these two things; they seem related. Here's the difference: When it comes to breakfast of bacon and eggs, the chicken is *involved*. The pig is *committed*. Commitment is a choice we make every day.

Don't Just Hope

A young, single guy had just entered the airport when he noticed a family waiting anxiously outside security. An attractive woman was wrangling her two small boys. The boys were straining and climbing on each other, trying to see around the barriers into the concourse. A cluster of people just coming off a flight appeared from around the corner, headed in their direction. The boys suddenly started jumping, calling out, "Dad! Dad! Look! There he is! Hey, dad!" A broad smile spread across the woman's face. Sure enough, a grinning, well-dressed man picked up his pace and emerged from the crowd. As his boys leaped at him like a couple of puppies, he scooped them out of mid-air, one with each arm, clutching them to him. He slid them down so their feet were on the floor, both still tightly coiled around his legs. He leaned in toward his wife, slipping an arm around her waist and planting a sweet kiss on her lips. They were all so excited to see him.

Intrigued by this happy reunion, the single guy walked over to them and said, "Excuse me, I hate to intrude, but do you mind if I ask…How long have you been married?"

Still gazing into his wife's eyes, the father answered, "12 years."

The single guy said, "Wow! How long were you gone on your trip?"

The father chuckled and said, "A long time. Two days."

The single guy said, "I'll tell you what…When I get married and I've been married 12 years, I sure hope my marriage is like that."

The father turned to face him. He placed his free hand on the single guy's shoulder and looked him straight in the eye. He said, "Oh, no. Don't *hope*, man—decide."

When we see a relationship like that, we can't help envying it a little. But think seriously: what's keeping you from having it for yourself? It's a choice to love that way. When we express that kind of passionate love to the people in our family— consistently—they will respond in kind.

To Love is to Forgive

It's going to happen that things will come between you from time to time. It's inevitable. To say otherwise is unrealistic. Anyone who's ever had a roommate knows that when you live in close quarters with another person, you're sometimes going to find yourselves in conflict. People have all different sorts of personalities and coping mechanisms to help them deal with these differences. One of the most effective tools in your toolkit is forgiveness, plain and simple. To love is to forgive.

In Matthew 18:21-35, Jesus tells the parable of the unmerciful servant. A servant owes a great debt to his master, but his master takes pity on him and forgives the entire debt. Then that same servant immediately goes out and demands that another man who owes him repay him the debt. When he can't, the servant has the man thrown into debtor's prison. When the merciful master finds out, he holds his servant accountable. When we owe others—when we make a mistake and do them wrong— we want them to forgive our debt. But when others owe us, or wrong us, we often simply want justice. Of course, the point of Jesus' parable is as simple as the Golden Rule: we should treat others how we want to be treated. You should forgive your spouse at every opportunity, because, although you don't deserve *their* forgiveness, it is what you need.

For most of us, we got married because we thought that would make us happy. We fell in love with this person, and we thought that joining together with them was going to fulfill us somehow. But the truth is, God places us in marriage not to make us happy, but to make us holy. Any human being is going to let us down. They're not God. We can only find true fulfillment in God, not in another person. Whether you realized it or not, when you got married, God was ordaining that relationship for your spouse to help you become more Christ-like.

If you're married, you might want to just take a moment now to pray for your spouse. Between you, God, and your spouse, pray for them and forgive every past offense, every debt, and every offense that you might be holding. Forgive them the same way Christ forgave you. If you're not married, but you plan to be one day, pray for your future spouse. Ask God to make you into a worthy mate, and ask God to protect your future love from the world's influences.

Why Write It Down?

A lot of people believe that they already have a vision. They may have given a great deal of thought (and even prayer) for the future that they would like to have. But that's really nothing more than daydreaming. If your future is no more important to you than a vain imagination like that, that's probably enough. But if you're serious, if that's what you really want, if you truly want it to happen, you're going to have to actually act. Intentions don't really matter that much. There's a path that leads from where you are today to that place where you want to find yourself one day. To go there, you're going to have to take some realistic steps in that specific direction.

Habakkuk 2:2-3 says, "The Lord gave me this answer: Write down clearly on tablets what I reveal to you, so that it can be read at a glance. Put it in writing, because it is not yet time for it to come true. But the time is coming quickly, and what I show you will come true. It may seem slow in coming, but wait for it; it will certainly take place, and it will not be delayed." (GNT)

What You Want Most

Let's simplify this verse. It's essentially saying, "Write it down; it's going to happen." Wait for it. It'll happen. God's going to do it. That's a powerful concept. If we just write it down and wait for it, it will happen. This is a deceptively simple principle. The value of writing it down is summed up in this statement: If you don't know where you're going, any road will take you there. And if you're just going to go down any road, the one you're most likely to take is the easiest one.

Imagine that you're driving at night in a heavy rainstorm. You can barely see more than about twenty feet in front of you. In those conditions, typically, you're going to focus on the lines painted on the road. If that's all that you can see in your headlights, that's what you use to stay in your lane.

Now imagine that the road curves, but only very gradually. You continue following those lines, but you may not really notice that the road is turning. You started your journey traveling north, but slowly, slowly you turned, and now you're headed east. It happened over miles and miles, and you could only see a short distance ahead of you, so you likely wouldn't even be able to tell.

This is what happens to a life without a purpose statement. On a broad scale, that's what has happened in our culture over the last 20-40 years. Closer to home, that effect is simply a reflection of what's been happening at the level of our families. It's because we don't have a focal point far out into the future that can direct us where we actually want to go. A purpose statement helps you remain focused on what you want *most*, rather than getting caught up in what you want _now_.

My grandmother was 11 years older than all of her siblings. She was the firstborn child, the oldest, and then, 11 years later, she had three sisters, one right after another, each about a year apart. Why would that happen? She was born in Czechoslovakia, as her family had been for generations before her. Her father and mother—my great-grandparents—wanted to build a better life for their family, but they couldn't afford for all three of them to move to America. So, when my grandmother was about a year old, her father came over first by himself. It took him 11 years to save enough money to bring over his wife and my grandmother. That was not the ideal situation. If my great-grandfather was given the choice, he would have kept his family together that entire time. The only way he was able to follow through was that he was willing to sacrifice what he wanted in the *now* for what he wanted *most*.

Your Family Constitution

It may seem like a really intimidating task to write your family's purpose statement. *What if I mess it up? What if I dream too big? What if I don't dream big enough?* Before Kerri and I went away for a weekend to write our family purpose statement, I was really nervous. We studied a lot of Scripture in advance. We made a lot of notes. We planned out how we were going to try to attack it. We felt a lot of pressure, particularly since Greg and Rhonda had been so emphatic about how much theirs had changed their lives. But before we left, we told Greg that we were going to give it a try. He encouraged us, assuring us that God would speak to us. He reminded us of James 1:5, "If any of you lacks wisdom, he should ask God, who gives generously to all without finding fault, and it will be given to him."

And he was right. That's exactly what happened. That's exactly what God will do for you, too. I can say that confidently, because since 1997, I've seen him do it for thousands of couples. I'm amazed every time at how unique each family's mission statement is. God has a unique vision for your family that He wants to share with you.

Think of it this way: a purpose statement is your family's personal Constitution. A Constitution is basically just a written agreement. You negotiate together to make sure everyone is going to be happy, to get what they want in the agreement, and then you write out the terms. That way, when opportunities arise, when questions come up, you can easily weigh them against your shared values. You simply compare your options to your Constitution. If the ideas you have align with your agreement, then they're keepers. But if one doesn't, then you know that one's not for you. That's exactly how you use your mission statement in your family.

Once you have your mission statement in hand, all of a

sudden, the way you handle your finances, the way you accomplish your work, the way you decide whether your kids are going to play sports—you can line up *every* decision you need to make against what you yourself determined was most important to *you*. Every decision you make leads you in a direction toward accomplishing what you believe is your family's purpose in this life.

Elements of Your Complete Family Vision

You'll identify four specific pieces that together will comprise your Family Vision or Identity. The **Purpose Statement** is what you determine, or purpose, to do, typically containing some form of action. A **Vision Statement** is descriptive, drawing a brief word picture of what you expect the future to look like. **Family Values** are specific traits or characteristics that not only are important to you, but also will direct your daily actions. These are often in list form, possibly including things like integrity, fiscal responsibility, and punctuality. Finally, **Family Building Blocks** are particular elements or objects that help communicate your family's identity, both to others and to your family itself. Family Building Blocks identify what your family is about, and might include things like a favorite Bible verse, a family cheer, a favorite book, a family theme song.

Purpose/Mission Statement vs. Your Family iD/Vision Statement

Most people struggle to understand the difference between a Purpose/Mission Statement and a Vision Statement, so we'll start by clarifying that distinction. We'll use some examples and then break them down a little. First, here's the **Purpose/Mission Statement** for Family-iD Ministries:

"Empowering families to lay the foundation for many Godly generations."

Our Mission Statement is purposeful. Keep in mind that the key word is "mission." What's your mission? Our Mission Statement says what we want to do. Although it doesn't go into specifics about how we're going to fulfill it, it does identify a simple, direct action we want to accomplish. A Mission Statement is frequently longer than a Vision Statement—sometimes much longer.

Next, here's the **Vision Statement** for Family-iD Ministries:

"To see each successive generation of every family live more fully for God."

Our Vision Statement is the view from 20,000 feet. It's short and sweet, typically a single sentence (or less). For many families, their Vision Statement is almost a team rallying cry. (We'll get to several more specific examples next.) Your Vision Statement is a top-level phrase that answers: "If we live our lives in the manner that most defines our values, this is what the result will be." The key word for this one is "vision." What do you want to see? A vision statement is a bit of a word picture that looks into the future and reports back to you.

Your **Mission Statement** says what you **plan to do**.

Your **Vision Statement** says what you **hope to see**.

Family Values

Several years ago in Sunday School, Greg told me, "Mark, you need to go write 100 Family Values." I didn't ask him why; I just did it. Now, years later, I know why. People ask me and Kerri all the time, "*a hundred* family values! How can you even keep up with those? I mean, five or six is good for me."

I like to answer, "What about the book of Proverbs? Aren't there about 100 family values in Proverbs?"

The more, the merrier, I always say. Carrie and I like to pick at least one or two of the Family Values from our list and discuss them every Sunday on our way to church. You'll find that your Family Values actually offer many more teachable moments for your children than even your Purpose Statement will. Your Family Values undergird it.

Your **Family Values** are the **character traits which direct your actions**.

Family Building Blocks

Just as the name suggests, Family Building Blocks are

actually many different things. They may be Bible verses, theme songs, cheers…whatever you can create or find and "collect" that help you communicate your family's identity. Within your family, you'll use your Building Blocks to help your children understand what your family is all about. Individuals have different learning styles, so you need to have several different ways to share the various aspects of your Family Vision in meaningful ways for them. One child may gravitate toward cheers and chants, but another might be too shy for that. Another might really love music, and would enjoy a family song. Of course, a family Bible verse is valuable for everyone in your family. Building Blocks have the additional benefit of helping you share your family's identity with others outside your home.

Your **Family Building Blocks** are **elements or objects that communicate your family's identity**.

Samples: What You're Aiming For

Finally, let's look at several examples. You may want to refer back to these as you begin to write your own Mission Statement, Vision Statement, and Family Values, and as you write and gather your Family Building Blocks. It's important to point out that many of the phrases you'll see in the coming pages might not make sense to you. When you write each of your own elements, you'll use the words and phrases that mean the most to you personally. Because these are examples, they make sense to the families who wrote them. To keep them short, often the phrases that people use in their Family Vision elements are simply abbreviations, ideas, and snippets of meaning. And that's fine.

Also, as you look through these examples, consider each of these only as suggestions and as ways to pique your imagination. Each is intended only to give you ideas. Your Family Vision elements will not follow a specific format or fit into a neat little template. They're not formulas. Every Family Vision is unique. Yours will be unique to your family.

Don't be intimidated. *You can't mess this up or do it "wrong."* There's no such thing. Your Family iD will reflect what *you* value, what God is speaking to *you*, and what's in *your* heart.

Sample Mission Statements

"We are called to lead…
In our personal relationship with Jesus Christ
In our demonstration of family unity
In our service to others
In our commitment to instill this mission into future generations."
"To love each other
To help each other
To believe in each other
To wisely use our time, talents, and resources to bless others
To worship together forever."

"To create a nurturing place of order, truth, love, happiness, and relaxation, and to provide opportunities for each person to become responsibly independent and effectively interdependent, in order to achieve worthwhile purposes."

"God has given you gifts and talents. He asks for one thing in return: Develop them and use them to help others. Fulfill God's will."

"We are a family that desires to know and serve God by being thankful, diligent stewards of His provisions; by raising our children in a family that is both a refuge from the world and a springboard into the world; by helping them to know Him and maximize their individual gifts, potential and calling; by passing down Naylor Family Values: our belief in faith, family and freedom as a heritage to our children, and promoting and demonstrating those beliefs to the world."

"In Our Relationship to God We Value…

…God's absolute standard …prayer

...God's ownership of all things and our
stewardship of our things

...thankfulness (instead of familiarity)

...time with God
...our sonship with God
...confession (agreement with God)
...seeking God first
...tithing and offerings
...God's trustworthiness
...God's timing
...cheerful giving by revelation
...contentment
...giving of praise
...who we are in Christ (forgiven, cleansed, and perfect in his
sight)
...confidence in hearing God
...being debt-free (not a slave to a lender)
...righteousness that turns aside from evil"

Sample Family iD Statements

"Untamed faith."
"You first."
"Live, love, laugh, learn—glorify the Lord."
"You're a Robinson. Take the lead."
"To give of ourselves to others."

The Top 100 Gunn Family Values

1   Relationship with God
2   Our relationship with each other; spouse first, then children
3   Treating each other with kindness
4   Challenge each other to have a deeper relationship with God
5   Priority of our families health
6   Courting over dating
7   Home education
8   Classical music

9	Living debt-free
10	Missions and missionaries
11	Laughter, having fun
12	Respect for elders and others
13	Respect for others' property
14	Honoring those who are older
15	Honesty in word, thought, and deed
16	Time together
17	The Bible is the inspired Word of God
18	Memorizing and meditating on God's Word
19	The body as the temple of the Holy Spirit
20	Doing all in word or deed as to the Lord
21	Others being more important than ourselves
22	Family reunions/holiday celebrations
23	Not speaking evil against authorities or others
24	Realizing that all things are working together for our good
25	Considering each other's feelings before we act or speak
26	Education = foundation of all learning and knowledge
27	Treating others as we would like to be treated
28	Honest communication with love; speaking the truth in love
29	Having an interdependent family
30	Core of shared values that all of us embrace
31	Being quick to say, "I'm wrong—please forgive me"
32	Parents who are approachable for their own sin
33	Humility before honor
34	Realizing that a haughty spirit goes before a fall
35	Being teachable and coachable
36	Marriage = One woman, one man; marriage forever
37	Making time for each other and attending each other's events
38	Bravely facing the teen years; set expectations
39	Attending church and sitting together
40	Family Bible studies
41	Loyalties to each other; remaining loyal to a trust
42	Family nights; family slumber parties and games
43	Date nights
44	Mom and Dad's relationship as the primary relationship
45	First-time obedience, without backtalk, having a good attitude
46	Avoiding evil and every evil way; we turn aside from evil
47	The desire and power to do what God has asked us to do
48	Praying to Him and asking Him first
49	Acknowledging that everyone's ideas are important
50	Valuing the family vision
51	Valuing planned family events

52   Selflessness
53   Conflict resolutions above conflict avoidance
54   A corporate sense of responsibility to all members of the family
55   Recognizing that the family unit is more important than individuals
56   Valuing the writings and Christian values of our Founding Fathers
57   Acknowledging that all nature points to God
58   Patriotism: honoring the American flag and country
59   Acknowledging that all governing authority comes from God
60   Working as unto the Lord
61   Savings; building a financial foundation for many generations
62   Morality
63   Virtue before knowledge
64   Living close to parents and grandparents
65   Studying the origins of life (creation) God created all
66   Valuing the lives of the unborn, the weak and the sick
67   Getting a Ph.D. in spouse and children
68   Listening to each other—not just what we say, but what we mean
69   Birthdays and spiritual birthdays
70   The calling on our family to damage Satan's kingdom
71   Soul winning
72   Hating divorce
73   Fearing the Lord: Realizing that he sees all
74   Salvation for all family members
75   Always looking for ways to go the extra or second mile
76   Using wedding anniversaries to revisit and add to the family vision
77   Annual goal setting and vision building
78   Each family member keeping a time management calendar
79   Memorizing the Gunn Family Chapter: Psalm 25
80   Valuing others' time; being prompt as a way to show love to others
81   Limiting phone conversations with friends
82   Generosity
83   Giving out of our need
84   Vision, passion, discipline, and total commitment
85   Reading good books
86   Meeting good people
87   Taking advice from experienced people
88   Doing today what others won't do so we can have a better future
89   Treating each other and ourselves as we can and should be
90   Praising each other
91   Honoring those who have helped us shape our family vision
92   Pastors and elders of our church; God is the head of these men
93   Business ownership and entrepreneurship is a great gift to mankind
94   Serving others as the way to lead them

95   Agreeing in prayer with one another as the way to move mountains
96   Shameless persistence in prayer (Luke 18:1-8)
97   Discovering and speaking each other's love languages
98   Valuing a surrendered life over a committed life
99   Laying the foundation for many Godly generations
100   Acknowledging the free enterprise system as good

Sample Family Building Blocks

Gunn Family Motto
WWJD? - What Would Jesus Do?

Gunn Family Vision Statement
"Laying the foundations for many Godly generations."

Gunn Family Cheer
Way up on a rooftop, Bangin' on a tin can, Who can? We can!
Nobody else can! Go, Gunn team!

Gunn Family Verse
Psalm 25:12-13 (Amplified): "Who is the man who reverently
fears and worships the Lord? Him shall He teach in the way he
should choose. He himself shall dwell at ease and his offspring
shall inherit the land."

Gunn Family Pledge
I pledge allegiance to the Gunn family which God has joined
together, to be loyal to each family member,
To make my brother and sisters my best friends,
To avoid bringing shame to my family
By living according to the family values By God's grace and
power.

From this section, I'd like to draw your attention to the Gunn
Family Pledge in particular. I liked it so well that I simply
replaced "Gunn" with "Naylor" and taught it to my family. If your
family says that pledge together every night before dinner, I
guarantee it will build a family identity. It... just... works. ---
Mark Naylor

PART TWO:
WRITE IT DOWN
Part 1

Chapter 3: Capture What Matters

We're close now to letting you take your first crack at writing down some of the chunks that will ultimately give birth to your Purpose Statement. This will be followed soon after by your Family iD Statement. Four steps will lead us through these two pieces of your Family Vision:

1---Brainstorm your family values, gifts, qualities, and dreams.
2---Condense the key elements for your Mission Statement.
Formalize and arrange the key elements into a congruent Purpose Statement.
3---Derive your Family iD Statement from your Purpose Statement.

For this exercise, although you won't need special paper, it would be a good idea to devote only one notebook to this task. Any kind of notebook is fine—spiral, moleskin, 3-ring binder, whatever—as long as it's one that you're comfortable using.

We recommend that you write by hand, rather than on a computer. Study after study has indicated that something about the physical process of handwriting has a hard-wiring effect on the brain. In a very practical sense, writing it down makes it "real" to you, which makes it more likely to actually happen in your life. If you're just hammering away at a keyboard, the chemical changes inside your cerebrum will be far fewer than those resulting from handwriting. Romans 12:2 says (in part), "...be transformed by the renewing of your mind. Then you will be able to test and approve what God's will is—his good, pleasing and perfect will." According to this verse, if you actively "renew your mind," then you'll discover God's will. When we get closer to the end of our process together, you can type your notes into a computer to organize your final statements.

For now, we're only going to complete the first two of the above steps. But before we even begin Step 1, we need to go over a few principles that will help you make the most of your time writing. These instructions will remain important all the way through, until you actually have your Vision Statement in hand.

Get In It Together

If you're a husband and wife working together, **the husband leads**, and **the wife provides critical feedback**. If you're the wife, you might be thinking, *I'll be good at that because my husband's not too bright, and I really enjoy criticizing him.* That's actually not the kind of criticism that I'm talking about. (More on that in a moment.)

We have practical reasons why we recommend this approach. In our early Family Vision Workshops, we frequently observed this phenomenon: Dad would hand the pen to his wife and say, "Here, Honey. You write." Maybe you feel like you have legitimate reasons. Maybe your handwriting looks like a third grader with ADHD, and your wife's looks like calligraphy from an original medieval manuscript. Those are fine reasons. But Husband, you need to accept responsibility. Although this is certainly a task you will do together, you need to lead your family.

Critical feedback means helpful, significant, practical, meaningful participation. One definition of "critical" from Webster's Dictionary says "exercising or involving careful judgment or judicious evaluation." And that's why the wife's feedback is "critical": it's the kind that prevents words like "Harley Davidson" and "golf" from appearing in your family's generational mission statement. Seriously, working together in this way provides an exciting opportunity for both of you to share your dreams, your biggest visions for what you want your family to be.

What you will discover in this process...is each other. It's very likely that you're just about to remember all those reasons you probably fell in love in the first place. Both of you need to share. Allow your husband to lead, and you share your values and thoughts. The main idea in this process we're about to begin is to capture everything that matters to both of you. In a later step, we'll steer those ideals into your respective statements.

Your Family Is Fine

Maybe you don't feel like you have a "conventional" family. What exactly *is* a conventional family, anyway? You may be single, without a family of your own yet. You may be a single parent. You may have more than one family that you're trying to combine, whether because of divorce or other circumstances. It doesn't matter. Be encouraged: God will give a Family iD/Vision Statement to *any* family who seeks him. According to Romans 2:11, "God does not show favoritism." That's pretty clear just by itself; I really can't say it any better than that.

A single man with a vision becomes an absolute chick magnet. If a young woman learns that you have a Mission Statement, a Vision Statement, and defined Family Values, she's going to say something like, "I've never met a guy who had a vision beyond himself and the next three days. What planet did you come from?"

If you're a single person, you need to realize—you won't be able to complete your Family Vision elements yet, at least not one hundred percent. You're going to need input from the person that God will send you at some point. Your complete Family Vision must incorporate their dreams, desires, and values as well, or it's honestly only *your* vision. However, if you determine at the end of this process that yours is in fact complete, then perhaps God's specific plan is for you to remain single. But make no mistake: Even a single adult can constitute a family. You're a single, right? That counts.

Along those same lines, if you're a single parent, then your Family iD cannot be complete without incorporating input from your children, especially those 8, 9, 10, and older. You'll need their help to complete your family's Purpose Statement and Vision Statement.

If yours is a blended family, you may feel like you're already coming from behind. You have his, mine, and ours. Maybe you're concerned that even though you can plan your whole vision the way you want, you still have to send some of the kids back to their other birth parent for visitation. Nevertheless, these coming steps will be just as critical for you. Consider this truth: a skilled coach can draw kids from different backgrounds and different environments, work with them, and every day have to send them home, perhaps to less than ideal circumstances. And yet, when those kids return to him, they'll still be able to effectively fulfill their role on the team, particularly if he knows how to pull them together. And that team has an equal shot at becoming national champions. We'll address in more detail later how you can ensure that your whole family—no matter how it's spread out—functions as a solid unit.

Greg and I have seen family Vision Statements that incorporated both family names. That may sound a little odd, but why? Think about the business world. Perhaps you've heard of Smith-Barney. Deloitte & Touche. Merrill-Lynch. Metro-Goldwyn-Mayer is actually *three* families! Just as in business, two families can be successfully blended. Your two families just might be able to come together and create something even stronger than the original.

Brainstorm

You may want to use the suggestions and questions which follow to help you brainstorm. Of course, don't feel like you have to answer every question. They're meant to be thought-provokers. Use them to help you formulate your family's key values and beliefs, and to identify the characteristics that are most important to you. This process has no limits, no bad ideas, no wrong answers. Don't worry about spelling, punctuation, or grammar, and certainly not about complete sentences. Your purpose here is to capture as many of your idealized values as you can. Take as long as you need.

1. In *The 7 Habits of Highly Effective Families*, Steven Covey offers a great scenario to help visualize the future you want: Imagine a 25th family reunion. Now ask yourself the following questions. (Remember to write down your answers):

---What do you want that to look like?

---What will people be saying about the family?

---About each other?

---What do you want God to be able to say about your family?

Examples: Full of faith, very loving, models of integrity, closely knit, faithful stewards, safe haven, etc.

2. Write down the characteristics, traits, beliefs and dreams that *currently* define your family.

Example: "We have a passion for helping those in need."

3. Write down things that bother you as a family. This one may seem like a negative approach, but it's a proven technique to help you identify things that you're passionate about. Write the things that really get under your skin. Then later, go back and turn those around, expressing a positive action that they can lead you to.

Example: "I'm unhappy about the world's influence on our family…" **Becomes:** "My family will impact the world around us."

4. What are our family's most deeply held values and beliefs?

5. What are our gifts, talents, and passions as a family?

6. What kind of words do we want people to use when describing our family?

7. What character traits do we want our children to develop?

8. How would we like our family, relatives, and guests to feel when they enter our home?

9. If our family were absolutely perfect, what would its elements be?

10. What is our family's truest purpose?

Condense

Now that you've assembled a random sampling of the things that are important to you, it's time to combine, consolidate, and pare down.

Mark your best ideas. First, look for what's *most* important to you. Read carefully through your notes and mark the ideas and concepts that you feel most passionately about. Circle them, make a star next to them, highlight them, mark them with a different color—whatever works for you. Just clearly indicate your best in some way.

Mark out the phrases that are less important to you. Take the time to discuss these. This is where you'll really begin to identify your family "Constitution." Be sure that everyone's needs and values are all addressed appropriately. Your spouse—and your other family members—won't cooperate if they don't buy in, and nothing in your family will change. You're a bunch of Pilgrims on the same boat. As Romans 10:12 says, "Be devoted to one another in brotherly love. *Honor one another above yourselves.*" (Emphasis mine.)

Consolidate and combine similar concepts. As you're identifying your passions and filtering out the less important ideas, you'll most likely notice some overlap—some statements that mean the same thing, or are very similar to each other. Not only is that okay, it's actually a really good thing. It indicates that those concepts repeatedly came up during your brainstorming. That likely means they're really important to you. Where you see that happening, refine your passion statements by combining them. Don't water them down; clarify and expand the idea in each one. Just as before, don't try for complete sentences. Don't worry about structure at all at this point. We'll get to that later. For now, the ideas, concepts, and key words are the items most critical for you to capture.

Set your target. If you have a whole lot of ideas—what seems like way too many—then try to shave them down to just eight statements. If your passion statement list feels more medium in length, shoot for five really focused statements. If combining them begins to make them really tight, aim for three. Try to group your ideas by subject. You might notice that a few specific categories emerge. These are likely your key areas of highest passion, significance, and importance, and will help you derive statements of related principles.

Examples:
"Desire strong sibling relationships"
"Active service to Christ"
"Have a servant's heart"

That's it for now. We have a lot more information that we need to cover, and we'll also go into the specifics not only of how to build your vision, but how to rally your family around it. We'll revisit the notes that you've made so far, and you'll begin to see those take shape into a cohesive mission. For now, this process needs to percolate inside you. You'll find in the coming days that more and more ideas will continue to come to you. When that happens, throw a net around them (by writing them down). Keep referring back to the ideas that you've already captured, and you'll begin to see gaps and more relationships within your values.

PART THREE: LIVE IT OUT

Chapter 4: Build a Rabid Family

A boy, about 12 years old, was doing reasonably well in all of his classes…except math. For some reason, he just couldn't seem to wrap his mind around it. Seeking help from their circle of friends, his parents learned of a small Catholic school just down the street. Its reputation was stellar, both in academics and in discipline, so the boy's parents enrolled their son at the first opportunity. After his first day at his new school, the boy came home and said, "Hello, Mother," and promptly headed upstairs. She didn't see him again until she called him down for dinner. At the table, he ate his food in silence, politely said, "Thank you," cleared his place, and ran back upstairs. Every afternoon and evening, this same ritual repeated.

After about two months of this behavior, the boy returned home from school one day, report card in hand. His mother anxiously opened the envelope. Straight A's. Even in math, he had an A+. She told him how proud she was, and both could hardly wait for his father to arrive home from work so they could share the good news with him.

When his father came home, he also expressed his great pride. After a round of congratulations and positive affirmation, the father asked, "So what was the difference? Was it your teachers?"

The boy shrugged. "No, not really."

"Well, was it the textbooks?" his father pressed.

"No, sir."

"Come on. It had to be something, son. What was it?"

A little embarrassed, the boy stuck his hands in his pockets and stared down at his feet. "Well, when I walked in there that first day, and I saw that guy nailed to that big plus sign, I knew they meant business."

True commitment requires some action on your part…but it pays big dividends.

Let's have a quick review. Do you know where your special sheet of paper is? The one that's not white? (Remember, we call it "The Father's Blueprint" in our Family Vision

Workshops.) Please get it now. Have you written anything on it yet? While the things we've been talking about are still fresh in your mind, think back: was there any idea, any concept, that really resonated with you, that you still haven't written down? Something you think God might be trying to tell you, that He's trying to get you to remember? If so, write it down. And remember, just as important: also write down what you think God wants you do about it. Don't forget to continue writing down those things that jump out at you.

Superfan? Or Player?

Think about someone you know who's a sports team *superfan*. Maybe you consider yourself a fan of some team, but that's not really what I'm talking about. You know who I mean. This person has hats. Shirts. Posters. Autographs. They have mugs, plates, maybe even a lamp. The curb in front of their house is painted with their team colors. They watch every game, and they go to every one they can. They paint their body for games— even when they're just watching at home. They're planning to be buried in a coffin with their team's official logo and colors. That person absolutely has rabies for that team. That team is *their* team.

I have a friend who's like this about the New England Patriots. He once said to me, "Greg, you should have seen us on Sunday. We absolutely killed. We were moving the ball at will. Our defense was just a wall. We were awesome!"

I said, "'We'? 'We'? I didn't know you were French. 'We'? What, do you have a little mouse in your pocket? You didn't do anything. I saw that game. You weren't there. They'd never let you on the field. They won't even let you in the stadium. They don't like you. The only reason that team knows you is because they have a restraining order against you."

Okay, I didn't really say those things. But certainly I've thought them. If you were to say something bad about this guy's team, he'd slash your tires and run over your mailbox. Nobody talks trash about his team without paying consequences. He has a tremendous capacity to show loyalty for them. That team is a significant part of his identity. The team has done a great job building their brand in a way that he relates to. He identifies with them. He feels like he's a part.

Now imagine you could create that kind of passion, that kind of identity, around your family. Imagine how you'd feel about your spouse if everywhere they went, everyone they met, people unquestionably knew they were part of *Team You*. Imagine that your kids don't only *think* they have the greatest family in the world—they *know* it. Instead of dropping off your fourteen-year-old down the block from their school because they're too embarrassed to be seen with the rest of you, they hop out of the car right in front of the school, a big smile on their face, fist-bumping and high-fiving all their brothers and sisters, backing away from the car, pointing back at you all, calling out, "You're the best! You're the best! You're *my* family! We're Gunns!" (Of course, insert your family's name there at the end. We have enough mouths to feed already, and we're not accepting adoption requests at this time.)

You absolutely can have a family like that. The key is to build a family identity, a way to give every single member of your family a specific role to play, an important way they can contribute. If your spouse and your kids identify themselves with your team, they can become rabid fans. But they're not just fans. They're more. They're players. They're actually *on* the team. Your team. The defending champs of the Super Family Bowl title. You can make hats, t-shirts—even have family colors and a family logo. Why not? Make your family actually *want* to identify with your family. Give your family rabies.

Earlier, we mentioned how important it is that we share God's deeds with the generations who will follow us (Psalm 78:2-8). Now we're going to look at the other side of that same coin—at what happens when we fail to continue the legacy that God calls us to. God encourages us, giving us the opportunity to pass it on, but with the way we live our lives, many times, we pass it up instead.

Pass It Up…?

1 Samuel chapters 1-4 tell the story of Eli. Eli was Israel's

chief priest in a time when Israel had no king, and was ruled only by judges. As chief priest, Eli was the voice of God, the very leader of his nation. Yet his own sons, Hophni and Phinehas, did not know the Lord. As bloodline descendants in the tribe of Levi, and as Eli's sons, they pretty much automatically became priests in the temple. And they were one of the worst examples of nepotism ever. Charged with leading the nation of Israel in redemption and worship, they abused their position; taking advantage of the very people who were coming to them to get right before God. Hophni and Phinehas would force people who brought their sacrifice to the temple to let them pick over it first, keeping the best portions for themselves, rather than offering them in sacrifice. They even routinely sexually defiled women who served at the entrance of the Tent of Meeting. They were very wicked—and not the early-eighties, you're-an-awesome-surfer kind of wicked, but the "disgusting, filthy, disgusting, vile, evil" kind of wicked.

They were so bad, the Lord actually sent a prophet to Eli to tell him that God was placing a curse on Eli's family...*forever.* "In your family line, there will *never* be an old man." (1 Samuel 2:31, emphasis mine.) "*All* your descendants will die in the prime of life." (Verse 33, emphasis mine.) Those who didn't die were cursed to live out their lives in poverty. Forever. Brutal.

But the reason was not even that Hophni and Phinehas were so evil, as we might think. Through his prophet, God asked Eli, "Why do you honor your sons more than you honor me?" (Verse 39.) Don't miss this: God cursed Eli's family forever because Eli had neglected to raise up his sons in a manner that brought honor to God. Scripture offers us one instance where Eli talked to his sons about what they were doing wrong after the fact (1 Samuel 2:23-24). "Why do you do such things?" But there's no record of him teaching them the proper way, the honorable way, to behave in the first place. He taught them the family business (priesthood), but he didn't infuse them with his passion for God. And it cost him for generations.

At about the same time all of these other things were happening, God sent Samuel into Eli's house. Hannah was a woman who deeply loved God, sorrowful because she couldn't have children. She prayed, crying out to her heavenly Father, asking him to bless her with a son. God granted her request, giving her a child. She named him Samuel, which means, according to Scripture, "Because I asked the Lord for him." (1 Samuel 1:20) Knowing that Samuel was her gift from God, she dedicated him right back to God. As soon as the boy was weaned, she brought him to the temple, presenting him as a servant to Eli, to be raised there.

From very early in his life, little Samuel was set apart as unique by God. At a time when God was not speaking very much to His people (1 Samuel 3:1), he spoke to Samuel (1 Samuel 3:8-10). This very incident was probably the defining moment of his life; the Lord called to the young boy in the night, confirming to him that indeed, the curse He had earlier pronounced upon Eli's family would come about. Samuel had to make the choice to share God's word with Eli, even though it was a hard word, and Eli was his mentor. (1 Samuel 3:14-18)

Years and years later, in 1 Samuel 8, Samuel had grown up, had sons of his own, and had grown old. Samuel had been God's voice to Israel throughout his lifetime. He had been the man of God, the very man who anointed David as king of Israel. *King David!* But as 1 Samuel 8:1-3 records, Samuel appointed his sons, Joel and Abijah, as judges for Israel. "But his sons did not walk in his ways. They turned aside after dishonest gain and accepted bribes and perverted justice." Dishonest gain? Bribes? Perverted justice? Maybe you're thinking, *No. Wait a minute! Not Samuel's kids. How could that be?* Samuel was a human being who was intimate with God. He literally heard God's voice speaking directly to him. Proverbs 22:6 says, "Train a child in the way he should go, and when he is old he will not turn from it." Although that verse would not be written until after Samuel's time, it seems impossible that Samuel, with his close relationship to God, wouldn't know that he was supposed to train up his kids. But Samuel passed up that opportunity. He taught his sons the logical extension of the family's vocational ministry (judgment), but he did so without infusing them with a passion for their mission.

Before you're too hard on Samuel, think about the parenting model that he had lived under. From the time he was scarcely more than an infant, he had been raised by Eli. Eli was like Samuel's father, and yet here was the same man who had failed to raise Hophni and Phinehas, his own birth sons. Eli was well-equipped to teach Samuel the temple rules. He even guided Samuel in the intricacies of listening for God's voice and obeying it. But he was simply not a good dad.

Ironically, both Eli and Samuel had right motives. But they both lacked the right methods. We can safely assume that both of these men *wanted* their sons to grow up to serve the Lord in a more powerful way than either of them had. But they didn't know how to make that happen. Andy Stanley said once, "It doesn't matter if your plan is to go to Florida. You can put on your sunglasses and pack your swimsuit and sunscreen. You can call ahead and make your hotel reservations. But if you start out in Atlanta and hop on I-75—headed north—you'll *never* reach the Sunshine State." Your intentions don't matter. Your direction matters. You need a map…and you need to *use* that map.

Recent polls have shown that the modern American family rarely plans financially further into the future than about two paychecks. Two paychecks! Maybe if you're really studious, you'll start thinking ahead about five years. That would make you unusual among American families. Well, how about 200 years? I wonder if Eli's story could have ended differently if he had thought that far ahead. I wonder if Samuel's might have, too. There's no question that these men knew God. There's also no question that their sons didn't. Eli's sons Hophni and Phinehas "had no regard for the Lord." (1 Samuel 2:12) Samuel's sons Joel and Abijah "did not walk in [Samuel's] ways." (1 Samuel 8:3) Why did these men disrespect their fathers and disregard their fathers' values?

…Or Pass It On

Eli didn't make his family attractive. His sons didn't identify with him, so they didn't identify with his values. Therefore, they had no reason to adopt those same values. Samuel made the same parenting mistakes with his sons. If your family is more attractive—far more attractive—than the alternatives that this world presents to your children, then they'll gravitate toward their family, toward you. Families require a healthy family identity to build that kind of density. Where family identity is strong, peer pressure is weak. Where peer pressure is strong, family identity is weak. If your family has more substance, more mass, than the alternatives, your family unit will have more gravity, drawing your kids naturally to your family, where they belong.

Fortunately, Jeremiah 35 offers us a terrific example of the power of generational thinking. This chapter tells the story of one core family who, for literally hundreds of years, was able to maintain God's call on their lives, passing on their passion, their zeal for his ways and his wisdom. Jeremiah 35 is the chapter that Rhonda and I prayed over during our very first Family Vision weekend, way back in 1996.

Jeremiah 35 tells the story of the Rechabites, an extended family who were descendants of Jonadab, their great-great-grandfather. Jonadab was alive during the reign of Ahab and Jezebel. During that time, under Jezebel's influence, Ahab was leading Israel deeper and deeper into idol worship (specifically Baal). Christians today would likely equate their practices with the sorts of things that one might observe in the Occult. Jonadab was able to foresee the inevitable demise of the family unit, which was gradually infecting and would ultimately decimate their whole nation. So he sat his family down and wrote a simple, three-part Mission Statement for them: "Our family will not drink wine, own a home, or grow crops."

Jonadab cast a vision for his family and established their family values in one fell swoop. His mission statement effectively rescued his family. Most of the temples to idols were built inside the cities. But because the Rechabites lived outside the cities, in tents, this helped them remain true to their Hebrew roots and avoid Baal worship. They weren't in a position to feel peer pressure from their neighbors. Second, their nomadic lifestyle helped them avoid major military conflicts. When Nebuchadnezzar, the king of Babylon, attacked with his invading forces, they simply packed up their belongings and headed for Jerusalem. They were herdsmen, generations used to living off the land. Because they didn't build structures, and because they needed to keep moving for their livestock to feed, of course they never even gave themselves the opportunity to grow crops. After just a couple of generations, these principles were not even particularly difficult for them to adhere to. Living in tents, not growing crops, and not drinking wine was simply their way of life.

In Jeremiah 35, the Lord instructed Jeremiah to bring representatives from the Rechabite family into the temple and offer them wine to drink. Jeremiah obeyed, and the Rechabites told him their story. Of course I'm paraphrasing, but they said essentially, "Sorry, we can't drink that. Our great-great-grandfather Jonadab told us not to drink wine, not to grow crops, not to build houses, and to always live in tents. And we've done that for hundreds of years."

The Lord was pleased to make a positive example of the Rechabites for all of the rest of Israel. They had faithfully followed their forefather's command for literally hundreds of years. Their vision remained just as white-hot after 200 years, as it was when their ancestor Jonadab had first spoken it. And yet the rest of Israel was too stubborn to listen to the prophets God sent them year after year, pleading with them to follow the Lord, obey His commandments, and avoid serving idols.

The Rechabites received a blessing from God that was almost the opposite of Eli's and Samuel's legacies: "…The LORD Almighty, the God of Israel, says: 'Jonadab son of Recab will never fail to have a man to serve me.'" (Jeremiah 35:19) God himself promised them that for generation after generation, *forever*, their people would *always* have representatives who remained faithful to God. What would you do to have a promise like that from God?

I want you to get at least two things from this illustration. The first is that it was not the Rechabites' specific family values— wine and building avoidance—that God was honoring. The values that were important to the Rechabites' family are not the same as our values. Certainly, Rhonda and I have clear rules in our household about the consumption of alcohol, straight out of Scripture. But it doesn't matter to me if my kids want to live in tents or McMansions. What God was honoring was not the Rechabites' specific values, but that they remained faithful to the values that their ancestors had passed down to them. This communicates to us that not only can you pass down family values literally for generations and generations, but that God honors us when we live this way.

The second important thing this story can illustrate for us is that if we're willing to follow God's specific plan for our family, if we're willing to passionately pursue what he places inside of us, then we'll likely look a little different from everybody else. In fact, we may look *a lot* different. Not only is that fine, but it's actually preferable. God has a lot longer view of things than we're even capable of. His perspective is different. When we do what He tells us to, without flinching on it, He can avert disaster for us, even generations before it presents itself. Their nomadic lifestyle contributed to the Rechabites' faithfulness to God. It helped them dodge the Baal bullet. It also helped them avoid enslavement to an occupying force.

Get Your Priorities Straight

When Rhonda and I read that promise from God to the Rechabites in Jeremiah 35:19, that's what we wanted for our own family. We prayed, "Father, please show us what we need to do in this generation to see you bless our family throughout every generation. If you don't come back for 200 more years, what can we do now to make sure that we will have godly descendants in every generation?" The first thing he directed us to do was to get our priorities in order.

It's been said that the best way to determine what's most important to you is to look at where you spend your time. After all, we only have so much time, so it stands to reason that what we do with that time would clearly indicate what we care about. That measure is quantity. How much time do you spend doing something? Each day is made up of twenty-four hours. The average person spends between six to eight hours each night sleeping. That's one-fourth to one-third of your day. There's likely nothing else that you commit to with that much regularity, and for that amount of time. So if quantity of time spent is the measure, then clearly sleep is our number one priority. But who would seriously say that? No one. We sleep because we have to in order to function. But sleep is not our number one priority.

Quality is of course another popular way to measure value. Let's say a man goes to a very nice restaurant, and after some consideration, decides on the $62 filet mignon. Some time passes, and the waiter returns...with a one-inch cube of steak, perfectly prepared, at the center of a large plate. The waiter smiles proudly as he places the flawless filet before the patron.

The guest is shocked and angry. "$62 for *that*? Are you kidding me? It's so tiny!"

The waiter responds, "Why, sir, this is the finest quality of cut available on the market today. What you are paying for is quality, not portion size."

"But I want both!"

We all want both. So when you're talking about the time that you spend with your family, which is more important: *quantity* time or *quality* time? Surprisingly, the answer is neither. It's not time at all. We've placed so much of our focus on time. But time is not the issue. We should instead focus on quantity and quality of *relationship*.

I have a friend who could have been the poster Mom of the Universe. Besides doing all the "normal" things that moms do— handling skinned elbows and knees, reading to her child, making sure he was clean, fed, and on time everywhere he needed to be—this mom took it to another level. Her son really enjoyed playing baseball, and he showed some early promise. So, his mom and her husband never missed a single one of their son's baseball. As if that weren't enough, either she or her husband spent two hours every day throwing the baseball back and forth with their son. *Every day*. They tried to split the time, so they'd each have time with him, but if anything kept either of them from that, the other would make sure it happened.

Clearly, they loved their son and wanted what was best for him. However, their focus was almost entirely on the time they spent with him. There's no doubt they provided him with sufficient quantity. They were intentional to support him in the things that were important to him, so they had quality covered, too. But even if you were to accomplish both of those, it still doesn't speak to the quality of the *relationship*.

Imagine yourself doing that for your child. And imagine if, every time you throw the ball to him, he either misses it or drops it. On the times he does catch it, his form is sloppy. Imagine that he can't throw hard enough, or he can't throw accurately. Imagine if every time you throw it to him, you say something like, "You're terrible. Why can't you do this right? This isn't hard. Why are you so clumsy? Honestly, sometimes I think there's something wrong with you."

Every interaction like that would be gradually destroying whatever relationship we began with, breaking off a little piece of his soul every time. It's not how much time we spend with our kids, or what we spend it doing that matters. The relationship is what's important.

Priority 1: Relationship with God

If you have a relationship with God—any kind of relationship with God—it will influence every other relationship in your life. If your relationship with Him is suffering, then all of your other relationships will suffer as a result. If your relationship with Him is thriving, then all of your other relationships will thrive.

When you ask Jesus into your life, you're supposed to decrease, so that He will increase. (John 3:30) Even the Ten Commandments are about relationships. The first four are about our relationship with God: have no other gods, don't make graven images, honor God's name, honor the Sabbath. The remaining six are about our relationships with others: honor your parents, don't kill, don't commit adultery, don't steal, don't lie, and don't covet. (Deuteronomy 5:6-21) Jesus made it even simpler for us: "Love God, love others." (Matthew 22:34-40) In this passage, Jesus said that loving God with all your heart, with all your soul, and all your mind is "the first and greatest commandment." Your relationship with God should be your number one priority.

In determining whether you're fulfilling that priority,

certainly time plays a supporting role. You should be committing time every day to being alone with God. How often should you talk to God? That depends. How often do you talk to your best friend? The more you communicate with someone, the closer you'll be to each other. How about this: "Pray without ceasing." (1 Thessalonians 5:17) It's as simple as that. Another place you need to set aside time for Him is in worshiping with others. Whether that's a Saturday, Sunday, or some other day of the week, "don't give up meeting together, as some are in the habit of doing." (Hebrews 10:25) The Bible is really clear on these things.

Just as with your family, it's not just about time. The quality of the *relationship* is what's most important. Do you talk to God? Do you hear back from Him? Are you reading His word? Is it speaking back to you? Is He directing the course of your life? If you're in control of the decisions, and you're ignoring where God is leading you, then let me just say as respectfully as I can: your relationship with Him likely is not your number one priority.

Part of why your relationship with God is so important is that you should be the spiritual leader of your family, and your relationship with him directly influences that. You can't lead your family to someplace where you haven't been. You can't teach your kid to swim if you don't know how yourself. To lead your family in a having relationship with God, you have to have one yourself.

Men ask me all the time, "Greg, how can I become the spiritual leader for my home? What do I do?" That's a perfectly reasonable question. Sometimes they'll explain their confusion by saying things like, "My dad wasn't a spiritual leader for our family. I wouldn't even know where to begin."

The answer is deceptively simple. A spiritual leader is simply someone who initiates spiritual things in their family. Initiate prayer at meals. That doesn't even mean you have to be the one to pray. You can actually delegate. You can say, "Son, please pray and thank God for our meal." Congratulations—you just spiritually led your family. Initiate. "Hey guys, let's read the Bible a little together." Initiate. Take your family to church every week. Initiate. In the car on the way home, say, "Kids, tell mom and me what you learned about in church today. Let's talk about it." Initiate. "I wanted to tell you guys some of the things I've been praying about/reading in my Bible/feeling God saying." Don't overcomplicate it. Initiate.

Priority 2: Relationship with Spouse

The second most important priority in your life is your relationship between you and your spouse. And if you happen to be single, then you need to shift this into maintaining a healthy relationship with your parents or your siblings—those family members who are the most important part of your support network.

How do you demonstrate to your spouse (and to everybody else) how important your relationship with them is? Say good things about them. Proverbs 13:2 says, "From the fruit of his lips a man enjoys good things." Show them honor. Proverbs 3:27 says, "Do not withhold good from those who deserve it, when it is in your power to act." Say nice things about them when they're around, and especially when they're not. Don't say bad things about them, especially when they're not around.

I wonder how many negative conversations have begun, "Oh man, you'll never believe what my wife did last night..." The Bible suggests a different standard: "Husbands, love your wives, just as Christ loved the church and gave himself up for her." (Ephesians 5:25) If you have something unresolved between you, talk to your spouse about it, respectfully. It works the same way from both directions. 1 Peter 3:1-3 promises wives that they can win over their husbands without even using words, but with positive behavior.

When you speak only well of your spouse, over time, I can guarantee you'll see change. The philosopher Johann Wolfgang von Goethe wrote, "Treat a man as he is and he will remain as he is. Treat as a man as he can and should be, and he will become as he can and should be." Speak blessings over each other. Encourage each other. "Spur one another on toward love and good deeds." (Hebrews 10:24) Encourage your spouse to pursue a closer relationship with God, and support them in that.

Get Your Ph.D. in Spouse and Children

Getting a Ph.D. is hard work. Most of the people who go through it do so because they believe it will be worth it in the long run. In the same way, getting your Ph.D. in Spouse and Children will cost you in time and effort, but it will pay huge dividends—not only in your own life, but in the lives of the people who are most important to you.

If you're single, you should major in Parents and Siblings. If you're a single parent, God calls you to focus your family education on Your Children. If you're single and you don't have children of your own, then you should specialize in Your Siblings. A young adult with younger siblings has more influence over those kids in their little finger than a parent has in their entire body. The best way you can influence your younger siblings is to set an example for them by honoring your father and your mother, the first commandment with a promise: "so that you may live long and that it may go well with you in the land the Lord your God is giving you." (Deuteronomy 5:16) That's a nice reward that's well worth the effort.

Priority 3: Relationship with Children

To be close to you, your children have to know that they can trust you. All relationships are based on trust, and your relationships with your children are no exception. The best way to build trust is to behave consistently. Say what you'll do…and then do it. Matthew 5:37 says, "Simply let your 'Yes' be 'Yes,' and your 'No,' 'No.'" Every time we break promises, we break down trust.

Of course that's much easier to say than to do. When you inevitably make a mistake that harms that trust, apologize. Ask for forgiveness. Practice saying, "I was wrong." When you apologize to your child, expand on that: "I don't deserve your forgiveness, but would you please forgive me?" If you lead your children in humility, then they'll learn that behavior from you—just like everything else they pick up from you, good and bad.

Own your mistakes, in the same way you would want them to. What I mean by that is perhaps best expressed in how *not* to apologize. Don't say things like, "I was wrong, but so were you. Now please forgive me." Don't say, "*If* I was wrong..." or "If what I did hurt you, I'm sorry." You know when you were wrong. You know when what you've said or done has hurt them. Own it. You be the grown-up. "I don't deserve your forgiveness, but would you please forgive me?"

It may seem counter-intuitive, but admitting when you're wrong will never destroy your leadership role. Apologizing actually enhances your position by making the relationship mutually respectful. Don't let the enemy (or popular culture) convince you that humility will communicate weakness and water down your authority. The opposite is true.

Communication Is Relationship

Every relationship requires communication if it's going to last. Don't let that intimidate you. Communication is really just a fancy word for "talking." Talk to your kids. What you talk about with them is important, too. Verbalize your commitment to your family, to your marriage, and to each child. Do that constantly. You may not be aware of this, but your children and your spouse perceive silence as rejection.

I realize that not everyone is a verbalizer. It's important for us to talk about this is precisely *because* this doesn't come easily for a lot of people.

A man and a woman had been married for twenty-five years, and the wife had had enough. It wasn't that he was a bad man. He wasn't. He did the normal things that a good husband and father should do. She believed he loved her. She believed he loved the kids. He went to work every day. He took the kids to soccer games and piano practice. He cut the grass and kept the cars' oil changed. He never forgot a birthday or an anniversary, and he always had a card and a gift. He was a good listener. But...he hardly spoke two words a day. And she decided she was through.

She confronted him one day, "How come you never tell me you love me?"

He answered, "I told you I loved you when I married you. If it changes, I'll let you know."

Maybe your father wasn't a verbalizer. Maybe you knew he loved you, but he just never talked about his commitment to you kids or to your mom. That silence can scream rejection to a child. Mark Naylor is like his dad in many ways. His dad wasn't a verbalizer, and Mark's not, either. Consequently, he has a tough time remembering to verbalize his commitment. Mark genuinely, deeply, passionately loves his wife and his family. However, he'd never think to say it. So he took practical steps to make sure he meets his family's needs: he set his smartphone with notes on a timer. It beeps, he checks it, and a reminder pops up: "Say something sweet to your kids."

So he'll turn and say, "Kids, I sure love you. You're the most wonderful kids in the world. I'm so glad I have you and your mom."

Maybe you think that's terrible. But it's absolutely not. It's wonderful. His kids love it. His wife loves it. They respond. Do whatever you have to do to make that happen in your life. You cannot underestimate the power of life that's present in the words you say. (Proverbs 18:21)

A woman came up to me once after one of our Family Vision Workshops and said, "Greg, my dad showed me in a thousand different ways that he loved me—but I'd give up 900 of those just to hear him say it." This particular woman's dad had already passed away. It was too late for him, and for her to hear it directly from him. But it's not too late for you.

Ephesians 6:4 says, "Fathers, do not provoke your children to anger by the way you treat them. Rather, bring them up with the discipline and instruction that comes from the Lord." It's easy to rile up your kids. You may just think it's good-natured ribbing, but be careful: you may very well be breaking off little pieces of their soul. Instead, you need to be the positive example and the leader that they need. Another version of this verse (NIV) says "don't exasperate your children." Nothing exasperates them more than when the rules apply to them but not to us.

This is just as true for moms as it is for dads. If you haven't been a verbalizer, practice letting those positive thoughts flow freely from your mind, out through your mouth. Express your love, your commitment. If you're a single mom, an even greater burden is on you. Not only do you have to be the positive, stabilizing force for your children in your own household, but to help them form meaningful, healthy marriage relationships later in their own lives, you need to speak as positively as you can about their father. You don't have to lie to them. But focus on the positive as much as you can. The negative things will be obvious enough without you pointing them out. It's so much better for your children (and you) to be a light and an optimist. Speaking badly of him certainly will never change him. Remember Goethe: "Treat a man as he is and he will remain as he is. Treat as a man as he can and should be, and he will become as he can and should be."

Jewish tradition offers three deliberate practices that parents can use to teach their children key elements that they'll need to live as fulfilled, successful adults. In practice, this approach has the additional benefit of forging a bond between child and parent. First, children are trained how to worship God at home. Passover is one such example, allowing parents to model traditional practices of worship. Next, parents help their children discover their individual bent, or gift, as well as at least one practical way to make a living. For example, your child may simply love to play guitar. Dad would say, "That's great. We'll get you a guitar and some lessons and make sure you have time to practice. And you're also going to be a dentist. You can be a dentist who plays guitar." Finally, in a traditional home, the parents participate directly in helping their child find a suitable mate. While they won't necessarily arrange a marriage, they'll teach their child how to understand their own personal commitment to family values. They'll also walk their child through the hard questions they need to ask of that potential match. By the time they've completed the courtship process, they'll have no doubts about whether their chosen suitor shares their ideals. Although all of these are practical techniques, they have one main thing in common: the value of the relationship.

Teens Don't Rebel Against Authority

Think back: Was there ever a time when you were growing up that you were in rebellion against your parents? Do you remember why? What it was about? When Mark and I talk to parents about their children who are acting out, usually by exhibiting rebellious behavior, we always find the same thing: teenagers rarely rebel against authority—they rebel against lack of relationship. When teenagers have an absolutely awesome relationship with a coach, with a teacher, or with a friend, they're loyal to that relationship. They defend it. They'll do whatever they can to protect it. It's not the *rules* of that relationship that they value—it's the *connection*. Whoever has the strongest connection is who has the most credibility in their lives, and therefore the most authority and influence. If their relationship with you is broken, but they have a strong relationship with friends who are bad news, where will they turn? That's not a trick question. They'll rebel against the lack of relationship with you, not against your authority. Rebellion is the relationship barometer between you and your children.

I moved away to attend college at a Christian school. Even at that school, many kids were wild-eyed partiers. Sometimes they'd come to me and say, "Hey Greg, we're going out to party. You want to go with us?"

I had no intention of going out with them, but I was a polite kid, so I'd say something like, "Gee, I really appreciate the offer, but no thanks, guys."

I knew that if my parents found out I was partying at school, it would really hurt them. My parents couldn't see what I was up to. If I had gone out, they might never have known. But my relationship with my parents was so strong, so important to me, that I didn't want to do anything to disappoint them. Our relationship with Christ is like that. We don't obey God because we're afraid he might vindictively do something awful to us or one of our kids—we obey God because we don't want to disappoint him. We don't want to break our relationship with him. We love him. When we rebel against God, we're not rebelling against His authority. We rebel against him only because we lack a relationship with Him.

What God Won't Do

I've known people who've gone through phases in their lives where they worked as hard as they could, putting in 80 to 100 hours a week on the job. And their motives were pure. They believed so much in the work of God that they wanted to earn as much money as they could, so they could give it to the church and to missions. Because they were using their God-given ability to make money, they believed that God would honor that effort and fill in the blanks for them. One man I knew believed that in his absence, God would be a father to his children, and a husband to his wife.

I know how he felt. Owning my own business keeps me really busy. It's always been important to me to provide for my family as well as I can. But occasionally, I'm torn. I know there are people out there who are involved in full-time vocational ministry, and honestly, I'm a little jealous of them. The fields are white with harvest. There's so much work to be done, and they get to use their gifts and talents on a daily basis to expand God's kingdom on this earth. I find myself thinking, *If I really, really sold out and totally dedicated myself to my church, if I serve God with my whole life, He'll understand if I'm not home as much. He's kind of obligated to pick up the slack for me.*

Here's what I've observed: God doesn't take up the slack for us. The only reason we think he might is if we try to change the rules—*his* rules. But the Bible is pretty clear about how we can get to know him. I've recognized three primary areas where God won't fill in on our behalf. We absolutely must:

*Spend time reading God's word and in prayer.** You can't delegate those tasks. You can't pay someone to do these for you. To have a genuine relationship with God, these things are not optional, and they won't take care of themselves.

*Be a spouse.** God will not be a surrogate spouse in your place. He will not be a husband to your wife, or a wife to your husband. If you don't do it, it simply will remain undone. God will be a husband to the widow, yes. But you're alive. Your spouse isn't a widow.

*Be a parent.** God will not be a father or a mother to your children. He's not going to read to your children at night. He won't teach them to tie their shoelaces and brush their teeth. Just as he fills the empty role of husband to a widow, God will also be a father to the orphan. But you're alive. Your kids aren't orphans.

God does, however, do something I wouldn't have anticipated with my limited human mind. If you're faithful to fulfill these other three obligations, God will absolutely pick up the slack for you at work. He makes things happen at work that on your behalf you couldn't possibly have put together yourself. But of course trusting Him to do this requires faith. The Bible says that it's impossible to please him without faith. (Hebrews 11:6) This defies logic. Luke 5:1-11 tells the story of Jesus telling Simon, James and John to drop their fishing nets on the other side of their boat. What Jesus told them to do didn't make any sense, but they did it anyway, and drew in the biggest catch they'd ever had. You have to trust God, even when—perhaps especially when—He leads you to do unusual things. Remember: Doing unusual things yields uncommon results.

Priority 4: Your Life's Message

You're building your life's message, even at this moment. God ordained every experience of your life for two things: your good and His glory (and not in that order). An experience may be good or bad—and each of us has certainly endured some really bad experiences in our lives—but God will use every one of those to construct your life story. No one knows what's in a person's heart but God. (1 Samuel 16:7) People can't read your mind. But they *can* look into your life and read the message they find there. They'll be able to look at the things you've done, the places you've been, the decisions you've made, and draw some conclusions about what's been important to you and what your character is like. To capture your child's or your spouse's heart, you must make your life's message compelling. Then they will be excited to participate in your story.

If you can remain focused on your top two priorities (God and your spouse), you'll discover that the way your message deepens is through trials. If you've already suffered a lot in your life, then your message is likely pretty deep. That doesn't sound like good news. But if you'll take the time, stay the course, and keep that commitment to get your Ph.D. in Spouse and Children, your message will grow powerful for touching people's lives. Think about it. When you face a complicated situation in your life, whose advice do you seek? The person I want to talk to, to listen to, to learn from, is the one who's been there. If I know who's endured incredible trials and unbelievable suffering—and yet has managed to maintain his priorities in order—that's whose words matter to me. His message is the story I want to read. I'll value what they have to say. Their wisdom is practical.

1 Peter 4:1-2 probably explains best why we should try to think this way: "since Christ suffered in his body, arm yourselves also with the same attitude, because he who has suffered in his body is done with sin. As a result, he does not live the rest of his earthly life for evil human desires, but rather for the will of God." That's great advice. If you're willing to endure the pain, then you'll live your life for the things that matter to God.

Priority 5: Your Ministry or Business

Literally billions of people on this planet have never been to church. But of all those people, most actually go to the same place every day, five days a week, for eight hours at a time: work. They may not go to church, but they do go to work. Your greatest potential for influence is not within the four walls of your church; it's at your job. Jesus told his disciples that he'd make them fishers of men. (Matthew 4:18-20) The non-believer fish swim at work.

God wants you to be successful in your business because that can give you greater influence in the lives of non-believers. Your co-workers and your employees may never pick up a Bible. But they'll read the message in your life every day. The deeper your life's trials, the deeper your message will be, and the greater opportunity your ministry or your business will have to provide a Godly influence.

God calls us to be salt and light to this world (Matthew 5:13-16), but many of our families have been destroyed because they've allowed their priorities to fall out of order. They've lost their saltiness or hidden their light. They put their business or their ministry first. Ironically that decision first takes out their relationship with their family, and then ultimately their business, too. One of the highest contributors to bankruptcy in America over the past twenty years has been divorce.

You don't have to go far to hear stories of men who awakened at age 65 to learn that because they had dedicated their whole lives to their business, to their work—because they didn't keep their priorities in order—they're alone. Their kids don't like them. Their spouse doesn't like them. In many cases, when a man retires and is at home all the time, his spouse leaves because she can't stand having him around. That happens because they quit pouring into those relationships. They quit knowing their spouse and their children, and now they don't share anything in common except maybe an address. Luke 9:25 says, "What do you benefit if you gain the whole world but are yourself lost or destroyed?" (NLT) A man who possesses such leadership skills that he could captivate the entire world would never lack for speaking engagements. People would travel from all over the world to learn his secrets for success. And they would follow his advice right down the same path to their own self-destruction.

I can really only think of one thing worse: to get to see the entire world come to Christ...and lose my own kids in the process. Imagine if every person on the planet had found a relationship with God, except for your family. Keep your priorities in order.

Matthew 6:25-34 promises that if we pursue God's kingdom and His righteousness (because our relationship to God is our number one priority), then He'll take care of our physical needs. Earthly "wisdom" tells us to follow that world-class leader, to listen to what He says and try to emulate Him. Godly wisdom tells us to ignore earthly things and give ourselves entirely to entering God's kingdom—that is, to finding that personal relationship with Him, being welcomed into His household as one of His adopted children.

Chapter 5: Independence vs. Interdependence

Imagine you've just finished getting ready for work. You're about to head for the door, and as you approach your spouse to say goodbye, they stop, smile, put their hands on their hips, and say, "Wow! You sure clean up nice. You look great today." They give you a nice hug, a little kiss, and send you on your way. Work goes on just like every other day: some ups, some downs, but you get your work done. A few funny things get said around the office now and then. Your spouse calls you a few times to ask your opinions on some decisions that need to be made. When you leave at the end of the day, you're looking forward to winding down at home.

You call your spouse before you pull out of the parking lot to let them know you're on your way. They say, "I hope you had a good day. I can't wait to see you." All during your drive, you're thinking about your family. Then, when you actually arrive home, your kids cheer, they leap up from what they're doing, and they swarm around you. They're visibly happy to see you. They show you the pictures they've made for you. Each one tells you about their day, and all of them want to hear about yours. Your spouse gives you their biggest smile and reminds you again how nice you looked today. The whole family settles down to a nice dinner together. As your oldest prays aloud, thanking God for their food and their family, you crack one eyelid, peeking out at all the wonderful faces around your table. You smile, and you think, *Life is good. Thank you, God, for putting these people into my life.*

Now let's imagine essentially the same scenario, just shifted around a little. You've just finished getting ready for work. Headed for the door, you approach your spouse and say goodbye. They continue getting ready, and without looking up, they say, "Okay. See you. Don't forget to drop off the dry cleaning." You grab your coffee and head out of the neighborhood. As soon as you pull out of the parking lot at the cleaners, your prep time begins. During your drive, you get your head in the game, mentally stepping through your day like you're heading into battle.

When you walk in the office, that attractive coworker says, "Good morning! Hey, those shoes are new, aren't they?" (They are.) "They're really nice. You know, you dress nicer than anyone I know." You smile and say thanks, and try not to linger too long in that gaze. During the day, most of your meetings proceed exactly according to plan. With each deal you close, you feel just a little more comfort, a little more positivity. Your spouse calls once right before a client meeting. You try to be polite, but of course you feel like you've had this conversation a thousand times. "Honey, you know I'm at work. You know they don't like me taking personal calls. Can't this wait 'til I get home?" Later, when you return to your desk from your meeting, your boss has left you a signed, handwritten note on his stationery. It basically says how great you are, how he wishes he had a hundred employees like you: "You were made for this. Your quarter looks like you're on track to break your own record."

When you finish up at 6:30, you text your spouse: "Headed to gym. Home by 8." During the drive home, you make a couple more phone calls to clients in different time zones. By the time you get home, you're wiped. When you walk into the house, the kids are in their rooms, playing, doing homework, or watching TV. Your spouse heads out for their turn at the gym. You have a salad before tucking the kids in and telling them each goodnight. You settle down to watch some news and you think, *Life is good. Thank you, God, for providing for me and my family.*

That first scenario is an *interdependent* family: everyone is looking inside the family to get their needs met. Picture them standing in a circle, holding hands, all facing in toward each other. As I've said before, Rhonda and I have seven children. I can't tell you how fulfilling it feels to have such wonderful kids, who are all happy to help out with family chores. It's richly satisfying to see your kids playing together—and not just getting along, but actually liking one another. They encourage each other. When one of my kids needs someone to talk to, someone to hold them, or just someone to hang out and spend time with, they all know they can count on me and Rhonda, and on each other.

The second example is an *independent* family. They all stand in a circle holding hands, too…but they're all facing out.

From a distance, you can see they form a unit, that they belong together. They seem connected. But if you look more closely, you'll notice something else. One spouse is looking toward their work for fulfillment. And not just accomplishment and success on the job, but everything: validation, positive reinforcement, self-worth—even identity. One of the kids is looking toward their friends for belonging, for people who understand them. This group's arrangement at home is more like roommates than like a family, with everyone doing their own thing. Sure, they're polite and courteous to each other. They're even reasonably respectful, working together to accommodate each other's schedules. But each person is focused on their own individual identity. Each one is looking outside the family to get their needs met.

Read Your Family

It's not complicated to spot symptoms that we're not meeting our family members' needs. I knew a family man who joined a softball team, and he just couldn't wait to get out to that field during the season. His teammates were always saying things to him like, "Man, we wouldn't even be able to compete in this league without you." The way his team valued him made him feel like he hadn't felt since junior high. Don't get me wrong: there's nothing wrong with playing softball. But there *is* something wrong with counting on that to fulfill your needs, needs that you should be letting your family meet.

The responsibility of meeting each family member's needs falls to the rest of us. We all know Mom needs to hear Dad tell her she's beautiful. And we all know that Dad needs to hear Mom tell him he's a stud. But there are more people in the family than just those two. Little Sister needs Big Sister to tell her she loves her hair—and to play with it. Dad needs to hear Daughter tell him she's proud of him. Son needs to hear Mom tell him he's smart. Big Brother needs Little Brother to tell him how strong he is. Each one of us is uniquely equipped and ideally positioned to pour into the people we live with.

If Little Brother isn't getting his needs met within his family, he has no choice: He's going to have to look outside. For example, if Big Brother beats up on Little Brother, slapping him, hitting him, pinning him, calling him "Idiot" and "Loser," Little Brother's going to go somewhere else to escape. He needs someone to tell him he's great, that he's going to be somebody. Little Brother is going to turn to friends to hear that. He's going to look to girls to validate him. Peer pressure will become the most powerful force in his life. To get what he needs from his friends, he's going to have to offer them something in exchange. He'll have to dress how they tell him. They'll tell him what kind of music he's going to like. He'll drink whatever they put in his hand. If he should get a piercing, they'll let him know.

Becoming a truly interdependent family requires constant vigilance. Loving your family means looking out for them. We have to pay attention to what's going on with our family members. If we notice anybody starting to gaze outward, that's our cue to start pouring into that person. Our family is in competition with the world—and we have to win. We have to watch for the telltale signs. If dad gets an accolade at work, we have to match it—or even better it—at home. If we notice Mom is starting to feel a little down, everybody should spring into action and throw an impromptu "Mom Is Great" party. If we don't rise to the occasion, the world will offer a counterfeit to lure them away. If we give our family the opportunity, the need, to look outside, the world is going to capture their imagination, and eventually their heart.

To fulfill each other's needs, we have to know one another intimately. Everyone has to know what matters to everyone else, what they care about. If one person's personality requires hugs and physical affection, then all of us need to consciously give it, and we need to do it regularly. If they value things that people give them, then we need to go out of our way to make them cards, write them notes, give them little trinkets that they can keep, that they can treasure. If they can live for days on a compliment, then we need to pay attention and graciously thank them for every tiny thing they do well. If they need time just hanging out together, then we need to get that on the schedule and make sure it happens. We need to swing with them on the swingset, read to them at bedtime, rock them in the BARCO lounger. We need to attend to their needs and do things for them. If you're not sure what works for a family member, then try a little bit of everything until you find what works. Make it family policy to know each other and to work to conscientiously provide whatever each person needs.

Sibling Rivalry...Or Sibling Revival?

If I could convince you to pass just one law in your family, it would be this:

"Every person in our family will treat every other family member better than they treat their best friend."

Sometimes your best friend acts like an idiot. But you're still able to extend them some kindness. Your shared interests and your shared history make it possible for you to find the grace to cut them some slack. If you can do it for a friend, certainly you have the capacity to do that for your own family. Most of us have experienced a boss or co-worker who was an "EGR": "extra grace required." (Many of us run into at least one of those every day.) Your spouse should receive at least that from you. We should treat the people inside our family better than we treat the people outside. That's how you create family identity. That's how you create interdependence.

Examples are all through Scripture about brothers and sisters treating each other badly. We're going to look at several now.

Cain and Abel

The world's first murder is recorded in Genesis 4:1-10, when Cain killed Abel. Here's what may be difficult to wrap your mind around: although these two young men were brothers, they didn't actually know each other. They were from two different cultures. They didn't speak the same language, and they didn't understand each other. What I mean is that Cain's lack of understanding was so profound that it led to him murder his own brother.

Your Brother's Keeper

Many of us grew up in homes where, although we may

have been discouraged from treating each other badly, we weren't taught that it was just downright unacceptable. I treated my little brother really badly. I was mean to him constantly, hurting his feelings at every opportunity. And it wasn't like our parents never said anything about it. They trained us. Every time I turned around, it seemed like one of them was saying to me:

"Leave him alone."

"Be nice to your brother."

"Don't beat him up."

"Give that back to him."

I also have a sister, ten months and two weeks older than I am. When we were kids, I craved her attention, even just the tiniest little shred of acknowledgement. I desperately wanted her to accept me. I wanted her to love me. If she had ever once included me when she had friends over, had just once said something like, "Hey guys, this is my little brother, Greg. He's great. He's really cool. Do you care if he hangs out with us for a couple of minutes?" I probably would have passed out. But instead, we'd fight and yell at each other. We often hurt each other's feelings, saying the meanest things we could think of.

In Genesis 4:9, the Lord said to Cain, "Where is your brother Abel?"

"I don't know," [Cain] replied. "Am I my brother's keeper?"

So much is loaded into that simple little question. Am I my brother's keeper? Galatians 5:14-15 actually answers that for us: "The entire law is summed up in a single command: 'Love your neighbor as yourself.' If you keep on biting and devouring each other, watch out or you will be destroyed by each other." The way brothers and sisters often fight, "devouring each other," they're destroying one another. I felt devoured and destroyed by my big sister sometimes. And I sure dished it out to my little brother just as badly as I ever got it.

Are you your brother's keeper? Absolutely, you are. From morning to night, 365 days a year, I am my brother's and my sister's keeper.

Jacob and Esau

Abraham received a promise directly from God: That the Lord would make a great nation out of his family, with descendants numbering like the sands of the sea, like the stars. Abraham's firstborn son, Isaac, received that inheritance from him. Isaac's first-born son was Esau, and as such, he was destined to receive the largest inheritance in his family. Although Esau was born first, he also had a twin brother, Jacob. Jacob tricked Esau out of his birthright, but even that didn't satisfy him. The firstborn son was also supposed to receive a blessing from his father, a purposeful family ritual, where basically his father would prophesy great things over him. But their father Isaac had grown blind in his old age, so Jacob managed to trick Isaac into giving him Esau's blessing. Jacob was his mother Rebekah's favorite son, so she even helped him to pull it off. (Genesis 25-36)

In that culture, the birthright and the blessing were the two most important things a man could receive from his father. Jacob's treachery would come with dire consequences: rivers of bloodshed for generations and generations. The unresolved conflict between these two brothers was passed on to their future generations. Some of Esau's descendants, the Amalekites, attacked Jacob's descendants as they fled from Egypt. (Exodus 17:8) The Edomites, also from Esau's family, refused to allow their Uncle Jacob's children to even pass through their land. (Numbers 20:17-20) Herod was the king who, trying to murder Jesus in his infancy, ordered the slaughter of every male Hebrew child two years old and under. (Matthew 2:13-16) Herod was a descendant of Esau; Jesus was a descendant of Jacob. One of Herod's sons was instrumental in the ultimate death of Christ.

God wants to heal the conflicts between us and our siblings. It is not His will for us to pass on the pain and suffering of our differences. Restoring relationships is important to Him.

Leah and Rachel

Leah and Rachel were sisters, married to the same man, Jacob. These women burned with jealousy, and had envy and strife between them. (Genesis 30:1-24) Children, and sons in particular, were critically important in their culture, and these two sisters basically went back and forth about which one was more valuable to their husband.

Joseph and His Brothers

Although he was the youngest, Joseph was his father Israel's favorite, and Israel made no secret of it. (Genesis 37-50) Perhaps understandably, Joseph's older brothers couldn't stand him. Joseph didn't seem to have a good sense of how to win their favor, either. He took full advantage of his prime position, even telling his brothers about a dream he'd had where they all were bowing down to him. That was pretty much the last straw for them. Their jealousy and envy actually drove them to want to murder him. Fortunately for all of them, his brother Reuben thought the better of it...so they just sold him into slavery instead!

David and Eliab, His Oldest Brother

When the entire Israelite army was quaking in terror of Goliath, the giant Philistine, only David, who wasn't even a soldier, was brave enough to stand up to him. (1 Samuel 17) Eliab "burned with anger" at his little brother for his courage, and he brutally chastised him verbally.

The Prodigal Son and His Older Brother

Rather than rejoice with his father that his little brother had come to his senses and turned away from his wickedness, the older brother was so angry that he wouldn't even go in the house. When his father came outside to talk some sense into him, the older brother took his father to task, judging his decision-making. (Luke 15:11-33) He was so consumed with himself that he couldn't see his way to forgive and welcome his little brother back home.

The Unkindest Cuts

Sibling rivalry has been widely researched and well documented in our culture. We're taught to just accept it as perfectly natural and ordinary. But God doesn't want sibling rivalry. He wants reconciliation, between us and himself, and

94

between us and our brothers and sisters. What God wants is *sibling revival*.

In our family, I was the firstborn son. My little brother Philip, the third child and second born son, had an almost insatiable desire to be accepted by his big brother. I didn't have any desire to even try to accept my little brother. Honestly, I just didn't see the point. But it wasn't simply a desire that Philip had; it was a legitimate need, shared by all second born. The second born child practically worships the ground that the firstborn walks on. Firstborns rarely possess that same kind of need for affirmation and acceptance. Nineteen out of the first 20 astronauts were firstborn children.

Because of the adulation that second-borns feel toward that older sibling, the firstborn is in a unique position to become the greatest mentor, the greatest advocate, the greatest cheerleader of that second born. Our enemy has been trying to pervert that position of prominence ever since man's initial fall. He places the evil desire into the first born to silence the second born. 1 John 3:12 cautions us, "Do not be like Cain, who belonged to the evil one and murdered his brother. And why did he murder him? Because his own actions were evil and his brother's were righteous."

This passage goes on to say in verse 15, "Anyone who hates his brother is a murderer, and you know that no murderer has eternal life in him." According to this passage, hate equals murder. That's because it's the seed, that thought we refuse to take captive, that will ultimately lead to some kind of destruction. (2 Corinthians 10:5) As we've seen, this cycle repeats itself all throughout scripture: Cain and Abel, Jacob and Esau, Joseph and his brothers, David and his brothers. But God wants to break that curse in your family. If you've seen this same pattern in your own family, let it end with you.

One evening after bath time years ago, I caught my little girl Hannah, our oldest, choking her sister Bethany. I stopped her; I sat them both down on the bed, and I said, "Let me tell you the story of me and my little brother Philip..."

My little brother Philip needed me to accept him so badly. He loved me. He would always say things like, "Greg, let's race!

Let's run!"

I'd say mean things back, like, "Loser! I can beat you. I'll always beat you. I'm bigger than you, taller than you, stronger than you."

We'd race. I'd win. And I'd call him "Loser," "No Good," "Scumbag," "Dirty Dog"—whatever I could think of. I'd kick him, spit on him, and push him down.

He'd say, "No, no. Come on, Greg. Let's run again! I'll bet I can jump higher than you!"

I'd think, *why does this twerp always want to compete with me? I'm bigger than he is. Why doesn't he get it?*

Philip just wanted me to accept him. He thought, *maybe, if I can jump higher than he can, he'll accept me.*

I hurt Philip's feelings at every opportunity. And every time I hurt him, I hurt him as badly as I could. I'd been downright cruel, on purpose. I wouldn't let him play on my team, literally or figuratively. I rejected him constantly. I was the main guy he wanted to associate with, to be like, and I rejected him. I drove Philip right out of our family, straight into the outstretched arms of his friends. All he had to do for them to accept him was to wear the same clothes they did, to talk like they did, to love what they loved, and to hate what they hated. That's all. They completely took over his personality and his identity. Peer pressure consumed him. He was not equipped to overcome it, because I had hurt him.

The One Rule

God is calling us to heal our relationships with our siblings. In our household, that means we must never allow our children to hurt each other. In our house, rejecting each other, hurting each other, is absolutely unacceptable.

After that choking between Hannah and Bethany, I told them, "Girls, there's one thing I will simply not allow in this house. There's one thing that's worse than anything else you could ever do: that's to be unkind to your siblings. Our number one rule from now on will be: 'Treat each other better than your best friend.'"

Did we still have conflicts? Absolutely. Of course we

did. Did we make mistakes with each other? Absolutely. You can't live in the same house with somebody without some conflict. But you *can* do it without being unkind. You can do it without hitting anybody. Through the years, I've occasionally faced conflicts at work, and I've always managed to avoid hitting anybody. I've learned ways to handle it with diplomacy, without becoming unkind.

Of course we have a much greater capacity for kindness within our family than we do in our work and other relationships. In your home, you should elevate unkindness between family members to the point where it is absolutely unacceptable behavior. Punishment for unkindness should be roughly equal to the punishment you'd receive if you tried to burn the house down…on the third try.

In my house, since we established this principle, have my children ever been unkind to each other? Yes. But the policy is in place. It's clear. Everybody knows it. So when it does happen, we bring down the law:

"No. No. That's not happening in this house. We are breaking the curse of driving siblings out of the house. We will not be an independent family. We are an interdependent family. Period."

This rule applies to everyone equally in our home. Rhonda and I have given our children standing permission to hold us accountable for how we speak. They know they must be respectful and treat us honorably, but they are absolutely allowed, even encouraged, to remind us, "Um…Dad? The way you just said that…would you say that to your best friend the way you just said it to Mom?"

Rhonda and I try to maintain a habit of humility before our children. I try to respond, "You know, you're right, honey. I was wrong. Rhonda, I was wrong. I don't deserve it, but would you please forgive me for the way I said that?"

Maybe when I was telling you about how I treated my brother and my sister as a kid, you were thinking, *Well, I'm glad I was never that bad. And I don't think my kids are anywhere near that mean to each other.* But the truth is, most of us don't realize how mean we actually are. Mark told me this story once about something that happened at his house.

One Friday night, two of Mark's daughters had a couple of girlfriends of theirs over to spend the night. These two girls are also sisters, and their whole family is just really precious. Both of these girls are really sweet and well-behaved.

A Naylor Dad tradition is that Mark cooks breakfast on Saturdays. He'll typically make pancakes or omelets. So on this one Saturday morning, he was making breakfast for the kids, and he overheard one of the visiting girls telling his daughter about her two younger brothers. She said, "My little brother Johnny, the one just under me, is a huge baby. He whines and cries about almost anything. But our littlest brother, Sam, who's four, is so tough, he won't cry at all."

Mark's daughter asked her, "What do you mean?"

She said, "Well, just the other day, I stuck my finger in Johnny's sandwich. I made the tiniest little dent in his bread, and he just started bawling."

Later that day, after their guests had gone home, Mark called his girls in. He said, "Hey girls, do you remember when your friend was talking this morning about sticking her finger in her brother's bread?"

They both nodded.

He said, "Well, let me ask you something. Do you think he was *really* crying over a little dent in his bread, like she was saying?"

They thought for a minute, and one said, "Not really. I think he probably cried because she was doing it just to be mean."

Mark's girls are so smart. She was exactly right. That little brother probably idolizes his older sister, and he just can't wrap his mind around why she would do something like that, something that was for no other reason than to just be mean. Is it the 50th little dent in the bread, or the 100th, or the 150th—before it just dawns on that little brother one day, *you know, I'm just not that close to my sister.* He probably doesn't even know why. It's not a specific event that he can remember. It was a gradual change over time, where his mind was re-mapped over time to avoid allowing her to hurt him.

The True Power of Words

Maybe you've heard that nursery rhyme that goes, "Sticks and stones may break my bones, but words will never hurt me." Let me tell you what words will do to you:

Words will burn, cut, slice, maim, poison, kill, destroy, and cause irreparable damage to you.

That's the truth. That version we learned as children was a lie. The Bible says in James 3:6 that "the tongue is a fire, a world of evil among the parts of the body. It corrupts the whole person, sets the whole course of his life on fire, and is itself set on fire by hell." That sounds pretty serious. Verse 8 says it's "a restless evil, full of deadly poison." Proverbs 18:21 says, "The tongue has the power of life and death, and those who love it will eat its fruit." The reason the pen is mightier than the sword is because words have started more wars than any sword ever will.

1 John 4:20-21 says, "If anyone says, 'I love God,' yet hates his brother, he is a liar. For anyone who does not love his brother, whom he has seen, cannot love God, whom he has not seen. And he has given us this command: Whoever loves God must also love his brother."

I grew up going to church. It seemed like we were there every time the doors were open. To get into the church, I'd have to step over the broken, bleeding, maimed bodies of my siblings. I cut them with my words. I'd physically pound on them. Then I'd head off to youth group to worship the Lord. I'd raise my hands, squeeze my eyes shut, and cry out, "I love you, Lord!"

This passage from 1 John 4 makes it pretty clear that I was a liar. I was a hypocrite. You cannot love someone you cannot see, when you're not even able to love someone you *can* see—someone who's made in God's very image.

If someone had explained to me what my responsibilities were to my siblings, I would have bought it hook, line, and sinker. In fact, I would have swallowed the pole, the rod, the reel and the boat. No youth leader, pastor, or Sunday school teacher ever told me what I've just told you. We have to teach our kids the truth about how they relate to each other. Each child needs to know and understand their role, particularly to their younger siblings.

Marriage School

The single most overlooked training ground for marriage is in our relationships with our siblings. Think about it. Your children won't have another relationship learning opportunity like that in their lifetimes. You have to live in the same house, share the same space, and the same bathroom with someone who's not always kind, not always loving, and not always mature. It's perfect practice for living with someone in marriage.

The way I treated my siblings, I was training for divorce. I was learning psychological warfare. And I was a really good learner. I could really hurt my sister. I could hurt her morning, noon, and night without even straining. I could hurt her when I was awake and when I was asleep. The truth is, if you can be kind to your sister, you can be kind to anybody. If you can have self-control at home, you can have self-control anywhere. That advice is stronger than forty acres of garlic.

Your Team Captain

The Team Captain is the most powerful position in your family. When I was playing sports, the captain had more power on the team than anyone else. A wise coach puts forward a team captain who has a vision for his team, and who can always keep the whole team in mind. A good team captain knows that his own fate is tied to the outcome of the team. In addition to that, the team captain is in a unique position of influence.

I remember one football team captain in particular. He was a senior, and I was a freshman. One time, after the coach had left the room, the team captain called all of us together. He said, "Look, guys, if me or my buddies catch any of you out partying during football season, we're going to have ourselves a little blanket party." At the time, I wasn't sure what he meant. But a friend of mine clued me in shortly after: A blanket party is where somebody throws a blanket over you, and then several guys beat the snot out of you. While you're covered in the blanket, you can't really fight back, and you're an easy target. That team captain had a tremendous amount of influence over the rest of us. Much more than the coach. There was no way the coach could keep us from partying during the season. But that team captain sure could.

Every family has a team captain. In the Gunn family, Hannah, our oldest, was our team captain while she lived at home. When Hannah got married, Bethany stepped into her role as team captain. You're the coach, and you need to pour into your team captain. You need to prepare your team captain to handle their responsibilities and to properly use their influence. You should take your oldest child on an individual outing, and explain to them their role. You should also talk to your other kids about the burden of responsibility that's on their team captain, and you should help each of them understand where they fit on the family team. If your oldest child is married, or even if they're single but out of the house, you should take them aside and teach them the principles of being team captain for their siblings still at home.

The Team Captain Pledge

What follows are the nine commitments that we ask our team captain to make. Together, these commitments make up our Team Captain Pledge. We actually have it written out and posted in our home. Of course you're welcome to adapt it or simply use it as-is. When you take your team captain out alone to explain their role, you should ask them to commit to these. You should also share their pledge with the other family members, so that they each understand what their older sibling is committing themselves to:

1. I will treat my brothers/sisters better than I would treat my best friend/s.
2. I will treat my parents better than my favorite teacher, coach, or superhero.
3. I will protect and lay down my life for my brothers/sisters; I will not step over their broken, bleeding, wounded bodies to go out and save the world.
4. My relationship with my brothers/sisters is a major priority–second only to my relationship with Jesus.
5. I will choose to resolve all conflicts, rather than just avoiding them.
6. If my brothers/sisters have hurt me in the past, or if they hurt me in the future, I will forgive and love them unconditionally–just as Christ loves

and forgives me.

7. I will conscientiously attempt to always set a good example for my younger siblings, as I know that they will be modeling themselves after me.
8. I will graciously accept the responsibility that my God-chosen birth order demands of me.
9. I will be mindful of how my words and my actions could be hurtful to my siblings, even though they may not be allowing their pain to show.

Of course, you can (and should) adapt these commitments to yourself. You can commit to treat your whole family better than your best friend. You can commit to treat your spouse better than your best customer, your best client, your favorite co-worker, etc. You can't lead your family to somewhere that you've never been. The best way to teach your children how to live is to live that way yourself.

If you're willing to actually do all these things you've just learned about, I should warn you: expect resistance. Some of it will likely come from your family, especially if you haven't already been intentional to try to live in this way. But just as much as that, expect spiritual resistance. I once heard my pastor, Craig Groeschel, say, "When God takes you to a new level, there's always a new devil." If you elevate your family to this new level, you'll need to be diligent to stick to your values. But you can overcome "because the one who is in you is greater than the one who is in the world." (1 John 4:4) Your enemy is already defeated. Let the sibling revival begin with you.

PART FOUR:
WRITE IT
DOWN
part 2

Chapter 6: Write Your Mission Statement
(More from Mark Naylor)

It's time to think about your special paper again, what we call in the Family Vision Workshop "The Father's Blueprint." If I were filling out my blue sheet, I'd write in big, bold letters: "Verbalizing." Greg wasn't kidding you; verbalizing is really tough for me. I have to write it down, schedule it, and remind myself to do it. I believe it's probably 40% DNA and 60% personality. Greg and I each have a lot of kids. He has seven, and I have six. But here's one significant difference between me and Greg:

One of Greg's kids asked him once, "Hey Dad, why do we have so many kids?" And Greg said, "Oh honey, it's because every new person brings more love for our family. God wanted us to have as much love as possible, so he gave every one of you to your mom and me. Each of you is a precious, special gift. I love each and every one of you so much."

One of my sons asked me once, "Hey Dad, why do we have so many kids?" And I said, "Well, it took me this many to find one I like."

(Just soon as it came out, I knew that wasn't the right answer.)

Before start writing again, I want you to first consider the value that your kids—and especially your older kids—might be able to contribute to your Mission Statement. You should try to involve your older children in this process so they'll feel invested in it. At the very least, consider their individual personalities as you're writing. That will help you examine whether what you're writing will stand the test of time with others besides yourself and your spouse.

Even younger kids have some pretty good ideas about things they think are important. When we asked some little kids for their advice about how to live, here were a few of their responses:

Ilene, age eight, said, ***"You can't hide a piece of broccoli*** *in a glass of milk."* Patrick, ten years old, said, *"Never trust a dog to watch your food."* Michael, age 14, said, *"Never tell your mom her diet's not working."* Michael also offered, *"When your dad asks you, 'Do I look stupid?' don't answer."* Katy, age seven, said, *"When your mom is mad at your dad, don't let her brush your hair."*

A Quick Reminder

I want to review once again why it's so important for us to write down the things that we believe God is calling our families to. Let's return to Habakkuk 2:2-3: "And the Lord answered me and said, 'Write the vision and engrave it so plainly upon tablets that everyone who passes may read it easily and quickly as he hastens by. For the vision is yet for an appointed time and it hastens to the end; it will not deceive or disappoint. Though it tarry, wait for it, because it will surely come; it will not be late on its appointed day.'" (AMP) If you'll recall, we simplified this before as: "Write it down; it's going to happen."

Remember the "rule" we used earlier: **the husband leads**, and **the wife provides critical feedback**.

Organize Your Key Phrases

Before we write the first draft of your actual Mission Statement—your family Constitution—we're going to tighten the key phrases that you wrote for Chapter 3, "Capture What Matters." Of course, you'll need your special Mission Statement notebook to write in. If you'll recall, you should have about five to eight statements to work with. Go ahead and find those in your notebook.

Narrow your key statements to a manageable number. If you have too many key phrases (eight or more), then carefully, critically compare them to each other and see if any of them are similar enough in character and purpose that could combine them. You may even find three of your existing key phrases that you can rework into a single, strong one.

Copy your key phrases onto a new page in a logical

order. All we mean by "a logical order" is one that makes sense to you. Maybe they'll fit into a sort of chronological order. Maybe you'd like to write your smaller ideas first, building up into bigger ones. Or you might want your bigger ideas first, progressing gradually down into more detail. They really could be any order that feels right to you. Don't worry too much about that at this point; of course you can change them at any time.

Mission Statement Guidelines

In just a moment, we'll refine each of those key phrases into complete sentences. Now that you've reviewed them and refreshed your memory, let's talk about some important characteristics that your Mission Statement will need to have. You'll want to try to keep these in mind as you turn your key phrases into the first draft of your Mission Statement:

Your Mission Statement states your purpose. This one might seem obvious, but it's important enough that you need to review it to be sure. The simplest, most basic function of your Mission Statement is to express, "This is what our family is going to *do*."

The Mission Statement communicates clearly and fully. When anyone reads your Mission Statement, they should be able to understand it completely, without requiring any additional explanation. Avoid jargon, or words or phrases particular to your culture or upbringing. For example, if you're a Christian who's been in church much of your life, you might be tempted to use words or phrases from the King James Version of the Bible. Or you might want to include an idea that's a complicated biblical concept. While it's fine to express those ideas in your mission statement, work to phrase them in contemporary language that doesn't exclude anyone from understanding it and doesn't alienate the very people whose hearts you want to win.

The Mission Statement should be timeless (generational). Your Mission Statement should set a realistic foundation for the generations who will follow you. For example, you wouldn't say that everyone in your family will become brain surgeons. A couple who were both youth pastors approached me at a Family Vision Workshop once and said, "Being youth pastors is so important to us. Can we put that in our Mission Statement somehow?" I told them that the significance of that ministry should probably be included, although not any roles specific to it. While not everyone in their family will become youth pastors, certainly they could focus their Mission Statement on impacting the kingdom of God through youth culture. Make sure it's both timeless and generational, in the sense that anyone in your future generations will be able to use it and relate to it.

The Mission Statement should include ends and means. Your Mission Statement should answer: What will we have at the end of what we do? It should also include means—in other words, how are we going to get there? For example, don't just say, "We'll be a loving family." Define how you'll know you've reached that goal: "We'll be a loving family by selflessly giving our time to the other members of the family."

Your Mission Statement should express not only, "This is what we're about," but also, "These are the results we'll see if we are successful."

Examples: Converted Key Phrases

Your Mission Statement will likely be several sentences, each one essentially an expanded key phrase. The best way to fill in the gaps in each of your key phrases to make them into complete sentences is to ask yourself: Specifically, why is this particular one *important* to me? As you answer this question, the words that you'll use will tend to become your ends and means for each key phrase. Following are some examples of key phrases that we've spun out into larger statements by applying the four guidelines:

Original Key Phrase:
"We want strong sibling relationships."
Becomes:
"We will purposely foster lifelong relationships between each other by making our brothers and sisters our best friends." Notice that it fulfills all of the elements of our checklist:

- *Purpose:* Foster lifelong relationships.
- *Communicated clearly:* Simple and direct.
- *Timeless:* We could do this for generations.
- *Ends:* Lifelong relationships.
- *Means:* Treat them better than our best friends.

> **Original Key Phrase:** "Active service to Christ."
> o **Becomes:** "We believe that each family member has a unique calling from God, and we will pursue that calling in service to Christ through a local church as well as a community ministry."

- *Purpose:* Pursue calling from God.
- *Communicated clearly:* States our value and direction.
- *Timeless:* Anyone who follows us would be able to do it.
- *Ends:* Pursue calling and serve Christ.
- *Means:* Local church and community ministry.

> **Original Key Phrase:** "Demonstrate compassion."
> **Becomes:** "We will expand God's kingdom by expressing Christ's compassion to everyone we meet."

- *Purpose:* Expand God's kingdom.
- *Communicated clearly:* Anyone reading it knows what we value and how we show it.
- *Timeless:* It doesn't exclude anyone in our family.
- *Ends:* God's kingdom will expand. *Means:* How? By constantly expressing Christ's compassion.

Christ's Mission Statement

Here's another important example, this one from Scripture. We consider Luke 19:10 to be Christ's Mission Statement: "For the Son of Man came to seek and to save what was lost." Certainly that's what Jesus accomplished not only in his time here on earth, but it continues today through those who follow him. In this one simple phrase, you can see his purpose, and that it is both easily communicated and timeless. To know if it meets the ends, you can ask, "Did the lost get found? Did the lost get saved?" Certainly, for those of who are believers, the answers are clearly "yes." Jesus conducted his means in the way that he lived, recorded for us in the scriptures. Because your purpose in writing your own Mission Statement is to pass your values on to your children's, children's children, you need to be sure that you indicate how they can accomplish these things.

Write Your Mission Statement

This is it! This may be the most exciting part of the process. Now that we've given you all the background you need, and you have your earlier ideas and key statements in place, you're ready to actually begin to funnel all those passions and convictions down into what will become the guiding principles for your family for generations to come. Are you ready?

Convert your key statements into complete sentences. It's a lot to remember, but as you write, try to keep in mind each of the key elements we've been discussing. Refer back to the earlier pages as much as you need to, especially if you start to feel like you're getting stuck. Also, use whatever tools you need. A thesaurus is really handy to help you choose just that right word that you may be grasping for. A dictionary is also useful. Certainly if you have a key family verse that you want to use as a building block, you can "cheat" by pulling from that.

Keep a record of the "Whys." One man showed Greg at one of our Family Vision Workshops that his Mission Statement included the sentence, "Each family member will feel loved and that they are important to the family." When Greg asked him what was behind that statement, he said, "I was the youngest of six children. I never had a birthday party. I went to my friends' birthday parties, but I never got to have one of my own. That had made me feel like I wasn't important in my family." For each phrase, as you're asking yourself, "Why is this particular one important?" you should keep a separate record of your answers, an expanded document of "Whys." Generations later, if your family can see why you included specific things in your Mission Statement, it will carry more passion and power with them.

Neither one of us will ever forget what that man said, so we'll also always remember that phrase from his Mission Statement.

Test Your Mission Statement

Once you start to feel pretty good about how your Mission Statement is coming together, read through it one time for each of the following three questions. Make sure that what you have addresses each one of these somewhere. Don't hesitate to continue rearranging the order of your key phrases as necessary.

Does our Mission Statement describe God's purpose for our family? If it does, then you're really close. If it doesn't, then your Mission Statement probably needs some more work. Be patient. Often, this process takes some time and prayer. But keep thinking about it. It will come to you. Don't give up. The gaps will fill in.

Does our Mission Statement express our ultimate objectives? There's an old saying when you're planning and writing goals: "Begin with the end in mind." Of course, we've already talked about including ends and means. This test takes those principles into consideration.

Will our Mission Statement hold up across generations? One key phrase from the Naylor family Mission Statement is that "Each family member understands their responsibility in training subsequent generations in the family mission." We included this phrase on purpose to let the people who follow us know that they have to keep this going. Of course, you don't have to include something as specific as that, but you do need to consider how your Mission Statement will continue once you're gone.

Tips for Tightening

We have just a couple more things you should consider as you revise your Mission Statement. It needs to be short enough that everyone in your family can memorize it. It also needs to be strong and forceful, with a sense of urgency and action in it. If they can't keep its core elements in mind, then it will be difficult for them to live it out on a daily basis. Consider these two tips as you review your Mission Statement:

Could I say it with fewer words? This is where a thesaurus and a dictionary really can come in handy. English classes we had in school taught us to write things in a very formal way that is more elaborate than we actually speak. You want your Mission Statement to have your voice, not your sixth grade English teacher's voice.

Are the words that we've chosen strong enough? Look first at the verbs, the action words. Use action words that express commitment, engagement, and passion. For example: we will, we believe, create, commit, grow, embrace. For the nouns, make sure that they're specific, and that they carry the full weight of the principles that you value. For example: unity, integrity, compassion, courage, zeal.

Keep Working on It

Allow the Holy Spirit to lead you. Allow Him to speak through your pen. Apply your own taste and your own writing abilities, and what will come out will be unique to your family. Over the years, we've seen many different structures for mission statements. Don't feel that yours has to match some kind of template or look like anyone else's.

Also, you don't have to feel that your Mission Statement is 100 percent complete today. Particularly if you've never thought about all these things before, your ideas will continue to evolve over the coming weeks. We usually recommend that couples spend intentional, focused time together to work on their Mission Statements. Make it a part of your regular date nights for a while until you get it where you want. Remember, Greg and I each took our wives out for an entire weekend to work through those first versions that we did, all those years ago. Don't feel overwhelmed if you can't get it all together in one sitting. That's not your ultimate goal. Making it timeless will take some time.

PART FIVE: PASS IT ON

Chapter 7: Make Your Family Attractive

The world acts like it loves your family, and it goes to great lengths to make itself incredibly attractive to them. It reaches out to each and every member of your family, beckoning to them with promises and good feelings. The world has spent billions in market research to determine what is *the* most attractive thing to both genders of every age group. And it continues to spend money trying to reel them in.

If your child is looking for role models, plenty can be found right there to tell them what's cool, as well as how to talk, dress, and act. Models for living abound; from 50 Cent and Snoop Dogg, to Britney Spears and Paris Hilton. If your child enjoys music—no matter what kind—the world has something for them. If your child enjoys fashion, magazines, TV shows, countless celebrities will cater to their fleshly hunger for the latest thing. And of course, sports have always been a go-to bad guy for examples of poor living.

When I was a kid, we had "Leave It to Beaver," "Andy Griffith," and "The Brady Bunch." Their storylines were positive, and their writers and producers were proud to play a role in trying to strengthen our nation's families. Of course, we all knew those were just stories. But so-called "Reality TV" has been remaking the entertainment industry for more than a decade. Now our kids can watch "normal" people become celebrities and see how other people "really live." You won't find any help raising a moral, decent, society-strengthening family from today's entertainment options.

Even though there might be some "positive" role models out there (assuming you're looking for them), that doesn't mean that they're programming your particular family values. The definition of "positive" changes along with society's mores. "Positive" doesn't necessarily mean "Christ-like." It doesn't even necessarily mean "moral," which could have been the simplest baseline fifty years ago.

Don't kid yourself. Stealing your family's heart from you

is big business. The world is experienced, and it's willing to spend, but what's perhaps more important, is that it's willing to keep up the assault on your kids' senses. That's where your responsibility comes in. If you want your children to absorb your values, it's not going to happen automatically. You're going to have to be intentional, and you're going to have to work at it. You may find yourself thinking, *How can we possibly compete with that?* Don't be intimidated! Not only is it easier than you probably think, it's actually a lot of fun.

We've already talked about the principle of building up your oldest child into a team captain for your family. That's truly the first key for winning (and keeping) your family members' hearts. When your oldest children believe in what you're doing as a family, they'll bring everyone else along. I'm going to let you in on a little secret: some people think a family cheer is corny. But my oldest two, Hannah and Bethany, knew how to sell ours to their younger siblings. Their enthusiasm turned the whole family into the Gunn Family Cheerleaders. Those girls make it look so fun, the younger kids think, *There's no WAY I'm missing out on this!* and they jump right in. That's because Rhonda and I told Hannah and Bethany the truth about the stakes, we kept them in the loop, we included them in decisions, and we gave them feedback and ownership. Once they understood the importance of their role, they were all too happy to use their unique positions of influence to help their siblings achieve their full potential. But of course it's not manipulative—it's simply deep love for one another.

The Closest Light

In 1954, Joe White's parents purchased Camp Kanakuk from its spiritual father, Coach Bill Lantz. If you haven't heard of it, Kanakuk is a sports camp in Branson, Missouri, that serves around 10,000 children every year. Joe and his family love the outdoors, and they spend as much time together outside as they can. In Joe's book, *Orphans at Home*, he tells a story about one night when he was walking hand-in-hand through the woods with his nine-year-old daughter, on the way home from a campout. The sky was clear and dark. Far from any city lights, they strolled into a clearing and were suddenly overwhelmed by a night sky with stars so bright they felt they could reach out and touch them.

As they stood there gazing, Joe pointed to one and said, "Look at that, Honey. That's the brightest star in the sky. That means it's the biggest, closest one to us."

A moment later, an airplane flew by with its landing lights on. He said, "Honey, which of those two lights do you think is the brightest? That bright star, or the lights on that airplane?"

She said, "Oh dad, those airplane lights are a lot brighter than that star."

So he showed her his flashlight and said, "Well, what about this? What's brighter? This flashlight, or those airplane lights?"

She said, "Daddy, your flashlight's a lot brighter than that airplane's lights."

At that moment, he realized: **The light that's closest to our eyes is the brightest light we see.**

Your family values might be only one candle strength, but if that's the closest light to your children's eyes, that will be the brightest light they see. When it shines right in front of them, it will capture their hearts and their imagination.

Love at Every Opportunity

I've tried to sell you on the idea of how important it is to have a family vision. I've tried to convince you that you need to enlist every member of your family in meeting each other's needs, so that everyone looks inside the family, rather than out. Now I want to tell you *how* you can do that, in practical terms. If you'll employ these techniques consistently and on purpose, the neighbor kids are going to be peeking in your windows, wishing your family would adopt them. Your kids' friends will constantly be begging to come over, and they'll behave like perfect little angels when they're in your house, hanging on the hopes that they'll be invited back.

Learn every child's "love language"...and then "speak" it to them. Author and counselor Gary Chapman has a terrific series of books based on the simple principle that we don't all experience love in exactly the same way. He has identified five primary means, or "love languages," that apply to most people. If you don't use the right love language with a child, even though you may feel like you're expressing love, it never reaches that child. (Bonus! It's also an extraordinary help to learn these principles and apply them to your marriage relationship.)

Find and take advantage of teachable opportunities, especially during non-conflict times. Deuteronomy 6:6-7 says, "These commandments that I give you today are to be upon your hearts. Impress them on your children. Talk about them when you sit at home and when you walk along the road, when you lie down and when you get up." It's easy to address character issues when somebody does something "wrong." You have to be more intentional to promote your family's values at all times. That doesn't mean you have to make an object lesson out of a peanut butter and jelly sandwich, but when you see an opportunity to share how God has influenced your family's life, you should tell them.

Vacations, hanging around the pool, and other special events are particularly great times to talk about what's important in your family. The positive atmosphere will make it stick, and the happy feelings will help them associate it with good times whenever they think about it.

Teach family values. Your kids will be more "successful" in the context of your family if you accurately set their expectations. They're looking to you to figure out how to "do life." Take advantage of their sponge-like curiosity. Tell them why you spend your money the way you do, why your schedule is the way it is, why you go to church, why you read your Bible regularly...and then be consistent, so they'll actually see it, too.

Have a family verse (and reinforce it). Speaking of reading your Bible regularly, there's no better way to teach your kids how important God's word is in your lives than actually living it out. Your kids could just memorize it like the Pledge of Allegiance, but it means so much more if it's something practical that they can apply.

Verbalize constantly how great your family is. Proverbs 18:21a says, "The tongue has the power of life and death." Be a verbalizer, Dad and Mom. Talk to your kids. Speak life to them constantly. What you say to each other is so important. Tell them how proud you are of them. Dad, tell the kids you think Mom's beautiful, and a great cook. Mom, remind them how much God has blessed your family with Dad. Say, literally, "We have such a great family!" We were fashioned in God's image. Your words create. Use them to speak powerful, fulfilled life into existence within your family.

Develop a supportive family community. Make friends with other families who are like-minded, so that you can uphold each other's values. At the very least, clearly explain to the people in your community of faith what you're trying to accomplish in your family, so you won't undermine each other's values. This is why it's so critically important for small groups of believers to "do life together." A huge side benefit is that your kids can see that your family is "normal"—that is, it's like other families they know. That reinforces your family values.

Include younger ones in the core family group. It can be a challenge to find games and family activities that include everyone, especially if the range in ages is broad. Be creative. In the next section, we'll tell you about some specific, unconventional games and ideas you can use. But even in the things you already do, you can find ways to keep the littler ones close and realizing that they're an important part of the family. For example, if you play a card game, put a smaller child in your lap and let them hold your cards. If you go to the pool, get in with them and carry them around. Don't only *think* about how special they are to you— *demonstrate* it to them.

To be fun, it has to be fun for everyone. Remember: God desires sibling revival, not sibling rivalry. Big Brother has Little Brother in a headlock when you walk in. He lets him go and explains, sort of apologizing, "I know I was hurting him…but I was 'just kidding.'" Whether it's playing a game, reading a story, riding in a car, or eating a meal together, it's essential that you enforce this rule in your home. The consequences for a child who suffers under others can last a lifetime. Here's a powerful corollary to that: The positive results for a child who is blessed and loved by their siblings will last a lifetime.

Model a constant attitude of happiness for others. Romans 12:14-15 says, "Bless those who persecute you; bless and do not curse. Rejoice with those who rejoice; mourn with those who mourn. Live in harmony with one another." Teach your kids to empathize with how other people feel and what they're experiencing. Do this all the time, but in particular, take advantage of the opportunities for this that daily family living provides. Celebrate each other's victories as a family. Avoid competition within your four walls. When one family member wins, the whole family participates in the success.

Lift up your siblings. Model for your kids how you want them to behave. It's easier to convince them that everyone should treat each other better than their own best friend if you actually live it. Especially if your siblings are all grown, reminisce for your children: Talk about the good times you had together growing up. Tell them funny stories about things that happened when you and your siblings were their ages. Avoid talking badly about extended family members in front of your children unless it's absolutely necessary. For example, if you have a brother who struggles with substance abuse, it's okay to tell them whatever's age appropriate, such as "he's not making good choices right now." But even in those circumstances, you can still tell them about the tree house you built together when you were ten.

Fun is as Close as Your Calendar

Unless you've already been doing these things for years, most of the suggestions and strategies that we'll offer to you are probably going to require you to make some adjustments. This next list goes a little farther. Some of these things will require that you actually schedule and plan specific events and conversations. Put some thought into it. Add your own twists that suit your family. You know your family better than anyone. Work together as Dad and Mom to make it happen.

Establish and maintain a "Family Night" one night a week. An absolutely minimum requirement is that you designate a specific "Family Night" every week, from now on, forever. Family Night occurs on the same night every week. We chose Wednesday night for our family, but you need to pick the night that's best for you. Family Night can be moved to a different night when schedules change (such as for school), but you must not neglect the sanctity of the event.

In 1954, my grandfather and my uncle started a car business, Diffee Motor Company, in Oklahoma City. I went to work for my uncle when I was in college. He took off every Wednesday. That was his day off. I remember thinking, even as a young man, if *I ever get to choose my one day off, I'm choosing Wednesday.* I like Wednesday because it gives you a break right in the middle of the week.

A little more than ten years ago, I finally reached a point in my own business where I thought I might be able to take off Wednesdays. I'm not going to lie to you: it was really scary at first.
I thought my whole business might go under if I wasn't there to constantly service it. But God has honored it, and it has become one of the best long-term decisions I've ever made. If my children have to wait seven days to spend time with me, their emotional love cups are absolutely empty. But every Wednesday, they know what's coming. That's *their day*, when Dad's going to be home all day with them, and it makes every other day go much more smoothly.

Find your day. It doesn't have to be in the middle of the week. But it does have to be intentional. It's a day that you don't work, don't focus on other things. It's a day that belongs to your family in the same way that one day a week belongs to church. Then, once you've established your day, protect it. Don't let anything get in its way. That one day will speak volumes to your children (not to mention to your spouse). It communicates extremely clearly to them all: *You* are my priority. *You* are more important to me than anything else.

Celebrate weekly game night. This can coincide with weekly Family Night, although it doesn't necessarily have to. We won't talk much about this here. We'll devote the entire next section to it, listing all kinds of specific games you can play and things you can do. We just want to mention it on this list, because you need to get it on your schedule. You should start thinking as soon as possible how you can make the games that you play fun for everybody.

Offer literal opportunities to practice righteousness on an ongoing basis. Pick a specific value that you want to instill in your kids, and focus on it for a week at a time. This could be "Honesty Week." Talk around the dinner table about the principles of honesty. Reward it when it happens. Next week could be "Humility Week." You can celebrate frugality, kindness, creativity, resourcefulness, etc.—whatever is important to you.

Plan a "Family Hour" *at least* **3 times a week.** Ideally, if you can manage it, you should have family hour every night, or at least every weeknight. "Family Hour" is a scheduled, regular occurrence that takes place as close to the same time every night as possible. It should take between 30 minutes and an hour, depending on what you do and how much time is realistically available. This is your family's opportunity to reconnect each day and love each other. For each night, focus on a specific theme, or set a regular schedule. For example, Night 1 may start with family prayer circle, followed by ten minutes praising God together, followed by each person giving a compliment to the person on their left, ending with reading a book or telling a story to the whole family. Night 2 could begin with one child praying aloud for the family, followed by everyone praising the Lord together through dance, followed by a family game such as "Socks Off" (see next section), followed by memorizing a verse together. Mix it up to keep it interesting, but lead: Make every Family Hour count.

Limit the amount of time your kids spend with friends. Mark Naylor instituted a weekly "Family/Sibling-only Play Day" in his house. His kids have lots of friends, and they're welcome to play with them—just not on that day. The doorbell would ring, one of his kids would run to the door, and it would be a neighbor kid: "Hey, can Johnny come out and play?" They'd answer, "No, sorry. This is sibling-only day. Come back tomorrow." If our siblings are supposed to be our best friends, they have to play with each other.

At my house, we set aside two weekends each month that are "Family-Only" weekends. Sometimes we plan things that we'll do together, like going to the lake, going to a park, or maybe going out to eat. Do whatever works best for your family. But set aside specific time that's just for you, without distractions and outside influences.

Make a secret "encouragement pact." At its most basic, we recommend that Dad make a secret pact with Son to say something encouraging to Mom every day. Dad is supposed to say one encouraging thing or offer some compliment to Mom, preferably in the Son's presence so he can witness it. Son is supposed to do the same thing, also in Dad's presence, so they can hold each other accountable. But it's a "secret," so Mom isn't supposed to realize it's intentional. Of course, you can also mix up this formula, so that it's Mom and Daughter saying something encouraging about Dad, Dad and Daughter saying something encouraging about Sibling, and so on.

A father who had attended one of our workshops told us about how he applied this advice. He told us his oldest son was having a really hard time being kind to his little sister. So, without telling Mom or Sister, Dad made a deal with his son. He said, "Son, for two weeks, you have to say something encouraging to your little sister every single day. I'll commit to saying something encouraging to your mom every single day. If either one of us misses just one day, then the two weeks start over again. And if either one of them catches on to our pact, the deal's off. But if we can make it all the way through two weeks in a row, we'll go to your favorite ice cream place, and I'll treat you to 'The Kitchen Sink.'" ("The Kitchen Sink" is a giant ice cream dish; they call it that because it has everything in it but the kitchen sink.)

The son agreed to the pact, and it started really well. One night at around 10:30, still early on in their agreement, the dad realized he hadn't checked in with his son that day. So he went to his room and asked him, "Hey son, what did you say to your sister today that was encouraging?"

His son said, "Oh, yeah. Look, Dad, I've been gone all day. I stayed after school and had a late track meet, and I haven't even seen her since this morning before school. Mom already had her in bed when I got home."

So the dad said, "Okay, well, get up, go in there and say something to her now."

So he reluctantly stuck his head into her room, asked her if she was still awake, and said there into the darkness, "I just wanted to tell you... you looked really cute in that shirt you wore today." Then he went back and got in bed.

The father and son managed to fulfill their deal, and it transformed the atmosphere of their entire household. His sister thought he'd gone crazy, especially at first—but she liked it anyway. The man's wife wasn't sure what to think, either, but it had the same effect on her. Father and Son's little pact broke the logjam they had been in. After that, it was easier for both of them to say positive things to the two women in their lives that they loved so much, and it didn't seem nearly as unusual when it happened.

We also particularly recommend this technique for single parents. Few things could be harder than to say something nice about your ex-spouse. But it's undeniable the positive effect it can have on your children to hear you say something kind about a person who's been mean or acted selfishly. It builds strong family identity, where your kids want to hang around you. They want to be in on what you have. They find tremendous peace in knowing that you're a positive person who always has such kind things to say. They'll trust you intimately.

Play "How could you have said that better?" This is kind of a game, although probably not one that you want to play 24/7. Everyone participates (including Mom and Dad), and we'll announce, "Okay, kids, today is a 'How could you have said that better' day." Then throughout that day, if you witness an inappropriate interaction, you get to call the person on it. They have to stop, take a few moments to collect their thoughts, and offer a better alternative to whatever they said. It helps your family practice holding each other accountable at a higher standard, but it's framed in a spirit of fun. Your kids might even enjoy flagging a remark that was perfectly fine to begin with, and the other kid will come up with the most over-the-top, sticky-sweet courtesy they can: "Why, dearest Bethany, precious sister with the most beautiful hair that has ever existed on this planet or any other, may I please borrow your fabulously stylish and tasteful blue sweater for the remainder of this most glorious day?"

Create special family awards. Mark's family has one we really like, called "Family Member of the Week." It's a special prize that goes to the child who invested the most in the well-being of the other family members. The whole family votes. You don't have to spend a lot of money to make these happen, by the way. It can even be a trophy that the whole family makes together, and it gets passed around from winner to winner. Think carefully about the unique personality blend you have in your family, and come up with appropriate prizes that will speak life, honor, and value to each of your kids specifically.

Celebrate milestones with memorials and special services. Take lots of pictures of a new home on moving-in day, and put them in an album. As soon as you're settled, have a party with cake and a cookout, inviting friends and relatives. Be intentional to help your kids understand why you're celebrating. When God does something unusual, big, amazing, even miraculous in your life, set aside a specific evening together when you'll memorialize it and celebrate.

Involve the whole family in giving to the less fortunate. Acts 20:35 says Paul said, "In everything I did, I showed you that by this kind of hard work we must help the weak, remembering the words the Lord Jesus himself said: 'It is more blessed to give than to receive.'" Take your children to local soup kitchens and ministries and serve alongside them. Explain to them the principles of tithing and giving offerings, and help them prepare theirs. In Alex and Brett Harris's book *Do Hard Things,* they tell a story about two sisters who started a ministry making small bags of necessities to give out to the homeless. The bags include things like a toothbrush and toothpaste, small nonperishables like energy bars and bottled water, and a short tract about salvation. They charge about $2 each (only enough to cover the expense of the contents) and make them available at their church and other places where people gather. People purchase them to carry around in their cars, so that when they see homeless people, they have something useful to give them.

Pray together. This is probably one of the most obvious things, but so many of us miss it. We get busy, or we just feel uncomfortable about it. But teaching your kids how to pray, and then praying with them regularly, not only connects them to God in a personal relationship, it also gives you a really good insight into what's going on in their lives and what's important to them. The simplest ones to keep on the schedule are meal times and bed times, but you can do more than that. Pray with them on the way to school, on the way to church, or on the way to family outings. You don't have to be fancy or formal. Focus on helping model for them a genuine, personal, ongoing connection to God.

Pray for your children. It *should* go without saying that you should pray for your kids every day—but I'm going to say it anyway. The most obvious opportunity is when you're praying together at one of the other times I mentioned, but sometimes you need to pray other things over them, maybe things that you don't want to say in front of them. I've done before something that I call an "hourly prayer alarm." I'll make a list at the beginning of the day of a few things I want to pray for each child, and I set my watch alarm to go off every hour, on the hour, with a reminder to pray. When it goes off, I take out my list and pray for just a few minutes and mark that kid off. That allows me to keep each prayer time focused on and devoted to just that one child.

Family Games, Activities, and Team Entertainment

Sometimes, when we try to think about how to entertain our children on a rainy day, we can find ourselves feeling overwhelmed. You may have thousands of crayons, markers, and colored pencils. Hundreds of coloring books. Boxes full of string, yarn, wire, buttons, beans, beads, and glitter. Gallons of glue. Pounds of play-dough. And still, you'll hear the children's united chorus: "We're *bored!*" It doesn't have to be that way.

What they're actually craving—which they honestly may not even have the vocabulary to express—is *time with you*. Interaction, engagement, with *you*, where you give them your full, undivided attention and interest. It's unrealistic (and unlikely) that you can deliver that on demand 24/7. But, if you're willing to schedule that time, putting it on your own calendar and on theirs, it gives everyone time to look forward to it, and you might be surprised at the creativity that pours out when everyone knows it's coming. But it's like periodontal disease: the time to start flossing is not on the day of your dentist appointment. Plan in advance, a little at a time each day, how you'll be prepared for the inevitable: that time that you *need* to spend together.

You don't have to spend hundreds of dollars buying new games every week. You don't have to subscribe to game and hobby magazines to keep up with the industry and all the latest trends. Certainly you may want to supplement your arsenal with those kinds of things, but you actually have hundreds of elements for game-play just lying around your house already. Ask any little boy: Almost any stick can be a "sword." If you're a little girl, every towel, bath mat, and random piece of fabric can be part of a party gown, just waiting to be discovered.

The ideas that follow are common suggestions, but they barely scratch the surface. You're limited only by your creativity. And don't just rely on your own abilities; engage your entire family in the brainstorming process. Become like a "MacGyver" family of gamers: Lay out all the materials you have on hand, and try to engineer an entertainment solution that works for your whole family.

The things we'll suggest here are all intended for use indoors. If you open yourself up to the possibilities outside, of course the potential just grows exponentially. We're being intentional about this approach, because you need a plan that you can execute on a regular basis (at least one night a week), regardless of the weather, temperature, or remaining daylight. It should go without saying that rope swings, balls, kites, and Frisbees are readily available—to say nothing of sandboxes, tents, and tree houses—so we won't dwell on those here.

Board games, traditional games, and bona fide "classics." Most of us remember at least a few games from our childhood. I remember when Trivial Pursuit was really hot. It even came in several versions, like Movies, Sports, and TV. Some huge games that almost everyone probably remembers are Monopoly, Uno, Skip-Bo, Sorry, Scrabble, Risk, Clue, Pictionary, and maybe Yahtzee. Maybe your family was into more traditional games, like chess, checkers, Chinese checkers, backgammon, mancala, Mahjongg, dominoes, card games, or even Bocce ball. Maybe you liked Life, Stratego, Battleship, Reversi, or Operation. What about Don't Break the Ice? Mouse Trap? Ants in Your Pants? And how about the all-time classics: Candyland, or Chutes and Ladders? Both of those were winners.

Puzzles. Your family might enjoy puzzles, perhaps of unusual shapes or complicated patterns. Sometimes puzzles are fun shapes of the things they're pictures of, like cars, animals, or even famous people in history. For little kids, you can find puzzles with simple shapes that fit into thick wooden cutouts. Some really fun ones even include magnets that let you "fish out" the shapes. You can choose to divide up a puzzle by color or area, assigning each family member with a different part, or just keep it a free-for-all. You can "puzzle race," where you time how long it takes you to work a puzzle, then disassemble it and do it again, trying to beat your time. You can designate a special "puzzle table" which always has a puzzle in progress on it, around the clock. A friend once told me about a genius neighbor kid he knew who liked to work puzzles face down!

Tent City. Did you know you can build "tents" in your house? It's true. You can move dining room chairs and other furniture around, hanging sheets and blankets over them, leaning big pillows and furniture cushions up against the sides, to construct enclosed spaces underneath. With careful planning and some clever engineering, you can architect a fortress, a ship, a palace, or a grand cathedral. Once kids build a new space, many of them like to "move in," bringing their bedroom pillows, stuffed animals, lamps or flashlights, and books and toys. You can leave a tent up for hours or days, even indefinitely, if you have a designated toy room in your house. Kids love to curl up together and be read to or even told stories you make up on the fly, about beautiful princesses and dashing knights, magical ponies and mythical armies.

Shared Storytelling. Set up a framework, where you explain that your family story will take place within a specific time and a specific setting...and those are basically the only rules. Flip a coin, roll dice, cut cards, draw straws, play odds and evens or "rock, paper, scissors" to determine who starts. Have everyone sit together in a circle, and determine in advance which direction the story will travel. A good rule of thumb is to pass the story in the same direction you play cards, typically to the left. Make it a house rule that doesn't change, so everybody knows in advance how this is going to go down. When everyone's in place, the starter begins the story: "Once upon a time, in a land called <u>some nonsense name</u>, a <u>hero/princess/warrior/dog/little kid/grasshopper</u> began a fateful journey." They get one sentence, and they can make it as long, detailed, and ridiculous as they can get away with. (Absurdity is encouraged.) Then the next person adds their sentence. And so on it proceeds around the family circle, with each person introducing characters, plot twists, new locations, or wherever their imagination takes you all. Your family's creativity— and sense of humor—will likely surprise and delight you. The adults and older children should take the lead in determining when the present story is about to run out of steam, and strategically use their sentence to end it dramatically. Then the next person in the circle gets to begin the next story, or you use your process to determine a new starter. (Bonus! This game works practically anywhere—including in the car.)

"Nic-pic." This is a picnic, turned upside-down and inside out. Picnics typically take place outdoors. Nic-pics are always indoors. Select picnic-style items to eat together, such as finger foods, chips, fruits, and small sandwiches. Prepare everything together as a family, just as you would for a "normal" picnic. Since you'll actually be eating inside, it's a good idea to keep some special considerations in mind to protect valuables like your carpet and laminate floors. (For example, you'll probably want to opt for plain water, rather than fire engine red Kool-Aid. Save your juicy watermelon for outside.) Lay out a blanket on the living room floor (or in any room of your choosing), just as you would if you were outdoors. Nic-pics take on a special charm when conducted by candlelight or other artificial light. You may even choose to reserve Nic-pics for after sundown. Enhance the fun by handing out flashlights to everyone, or by using a larger, lantern-style flashlight that you place in the middle of the group.

At least one family has even told us that when an evening storm knocks out the electricity, their kids freak out (in a good way), scrambling excitedly for flashlights and begging to have a Nic-pic. Combine Nic-pic time with other appropriate family games, such as team storytelling.

Mattress Night. Drag mattresses to the living room for a family slumber party. Tell stories about your childhood experiences. (You'll likely only need 4 or 5 stories because your kids will ask to hear the same ones over and over again.)

Tickle Jail. All the kids get together in one room. Dad guards the door and pretends to fall asleep. The kids try to "escape" from jail. Any kids that Dad "catches" trying to escape get tickled. If a child does actually escape, Dad has to hunt them down, subdue them with his tickle powers, and tickle them back to jail.

Socks Off. Lay out and clearly define out-of-bounds boundaries in a space large enough to accommodate all the players. You can do it on a large rug, or lay out pillows or cushions at the edges or corners. Everyone removes their shoes and wears two socks, one on each foot. They must lie on the floor and crawl, remaining within the boundaries. The object is to take off everyone else's socks, while keeping your own socks on. The last player who still has on at least one sock wins. Be sure you set clear parameters about kicking and other possible forms of cheating. For example, one of my sons once proudly swaggered into a socks-off competition with both socks fastened securely to his calves…using most of a roll of duct tape.

Paper Airplane Contest. Everyone makes and decorates a paper airplane, culminating in a "Throw-Off" competition, which should include prizes for the winners in each category. Clearly lay out age-appropriate rules for the competition in advance, such as greatest distance in a single throw, greatest distance for a combined three throws, straightest throw, prettiest plane, most unique design, etc. Parents or older children should assist younger children in method and execution in design, construction, and proper throwing technique. As always, make sure it's fun for everyone.

Only the Beginning…

What we've tried to give you in this chapter is just a foundation to begin building on. These are ideas that can get you started immediately enjoying your family together. Literally thousands of games and game ideas are available on the Internet. Simply search for "family games," "family friendly games," "party games," "games for children," and similar terms. Not only will you find games available for purchase, but you'll also find ideas, suggestions, and forums—even ways to connect with other families.

The only thing the world has to offer your children is shallow entertainment that appeals to their immediate desires. Your family can easily fill that space, and add to it genuine relationship. You can strategically build memories that your children will carry through their own lifetimes directly into their own families one day. Just imagine: your great-great-great grandchildren, long after you've gone on to be with the Lord, rolling around on the floor, laughing, tickling, and tearing at each other's socks. And it all begins with you and your children…now.

Chapter 8: How to be a Great Dad

Most of the ideas we've offered so far haven't been specific to one parent over the other. The whole family should participate as much as possible. In this chapter, however, we'll focus specifically on what Dad can (and should) do. Of course, Mom can do any of these as well, but Dad, you need to be really intentional to remain always connected to every one of your children individually. One of the most common hurts that people express as adults is that, when they were kids, Dad was emotionally unavailable. There's a line from an old comedy where a grown son shouts at his dad, "You ruined my life!" to which his father replies, "How could I? I wasn't even there!"

It's a funny moment when it happens in a movie, but the simple, poignant truth of it really stings. Even when we Dads are physically present, the things that can occupy our minds—bills, work, entertainment, sports—conspire to make us not "there." Taking the time to be intentional and give each child our full, undivided attention will do more to grow them into the well-adjusted adults we hope they'll become than even the nicest gated-community mansion, followed up with the finest Ivy League education. As simple as helping them with their math homework or reading them the story of David and Goliath from the Children's Bible, we can invest in their lives in ways that pay infinite dividends, both in their lives and in ours.

Connect and Invest

The most valuable resource on earth is time. You can always make more money, but your time is fleeting. Investing time in your children, participating in their lives in intentional ways, is the single best way to make sure you maintain healthy relationships. It will give you those necessary opportunities to speak into their lives. Here are several ideas you can use (and expand on) for your family.

Take your daughters out on "Date nights" and your sons on "Dad's days." Set a goal to take each child out individually at least once a month. If you have a daughter, take her out on "date night" where you spend quality time alone together and you can teach her the qualities she'll need to look for in a true gentleman: opening doors, tending to her needs, being a good listener, etc. And don't take her to the sports grill on the corner; do what *she* wants to do. If that includes dressing up, wear a suit and tie.

If you have sons, take them to events they enjoy. But be practical, because you have a two-fold purpose: to bond with them, and to teach them things they'll need to know: how be a true gentleman (see above), characteristics to look for in a godly potential mate, how to pay for things, etc.

These should be times that your children look forward to with great anticipation. Schedule them in advance, and keep your commitments. They don't all have to cost money, either. You can pack a picnic dinner and take your daughter to a park. You can grab a ball and a couple of gloves and take your son to a school playground for a catch. You can even take them to the library to pick out some books.

When Mark takes one of his daughters out, they get all dressed up. He'll wear a suit and tie, and she'll wear a dress and fix her hair. When I take my little girls out, I'll ask them, "Honey, will you let me be your boyfriend until you get married?" They love it. We hold hands and fuss over each other. Of course, they'll outgrow this phase eventually. If your girls are still small, though, don't miss your chance to be the most special man in their lives.

Prepare Saturday morning breakfast. A tradition for the Naylor men is to prepare breakfast on Saturday mornings. Mark usually makes pancakes or waffles for everyone. You can easily do the same. But you don't have to limit yourself to pancakes and waffles; become a culinary expert for your children. "Take orders" earlier in the week, and make sure you have all the ingredients you'll need for Saturday—whether it's special omelets, French toast, fried potatoes, biscuits and gravy, or a bunch of fruit. Invite the kids into the kitchen to watch as you prepare their food. Make a production of it. Constantly brainwash them, saying things like, "You know, guys, your dad's the greatest breakfast chef in North America, maybe in the history of the world." Keep it light, silly, and entertaining. Saturday can be "Mom's Special Sleep-In Day," where you make a game out of being as quiet as possible until she's ready to get up. A special side note here: don't let special breakfast backfire on you—clean up the kitchen when you're done!

Take your kids to work. My dad was a pharmaceutical rep for 25 years. Southeast Oklahoma was his territory, so he was gone for two weeks out of every month, sleeping at hotels. I *wish* my dad would have taken me to work with him. I would have put on a suit and tie like him. I would have shaken those doctors' hands and convinced them to buy something from my dad.

When it's possible, you should plan to take each child to your work at least once every school year. Of course, be sensitive to your own work situation. Schedule it in advance with your boss, and plan to only have them there for a half day or so (an hour or two for smaller children). Plan ahead, and bring "work" that your kids can do while they're with you. This is a teaching opportunity. Tell them about your job, and show them some of what you do.

Take your kids with you whenever you can. Plan strategically to take your kids with you anytime you have errands you need to run: to the home improvement store, to the bank, to the grocery store, to get the oil changed. Try to arrange tasks so that you get a double-whammy: give Mom some alone time while you're pouring into your kids. You can't always take everybody with you, especially if you have several kids. Be strategic, and take just one kid that you need to talk to alone, or take a combination of the kids so you can teach something through what you're doing. Coordinate with Mom to make sure you're getting the most bang for the buck. Remember, though: even though life is a classroom, "school" doesn't have to be boring. Don't just run your errands; "fun" your errands!

Prepare special outings. You can throw together picnics and gear for all sorts of regular time outside, as well as for special holidays and events, like the Fourth of July for example. Think things through. If it's hot out, be sure you pack enough water and cool drinks. If bugs or sun exposure will be an issue, be sure you bring enough insect repellent and sunscreen for everybody. Involve Mom only as much as she wants to be—your two-fold goal is to make special memories your kids will cherish, and to give your wife a break. She should be a passenger enjoying your event, with zero pressure for preparing it. The two keys to success here are (1) to plan ahead enough that you take care of everything, and (2) to always remember: It's only fun if it's fun for *everybody*—not just you. (Don't take the whole family fishing if you love it, but some of them hate it.)

Get the boys ready for church. Just as with bath and bed time, coordinate with Mom, taking ownership over only the tasks she's comfortable surrendering to you. (Helpful Tip: Then you must actually follow through and execute on these, including any specific instructions or guidelines Mom provides.) Let's say Mom irons and lays out their clothes the night before. Then on church day, you run Reveille, waking up and rallying the troops, making sure everybody uses the bathroom, everybody gets mess (breakfast), and inspecting footlockers (tidy closets) and beds. Then you make sure everybody gets shaved (teeth brushed thoroughly and properly) and in uniform. Double-check for clean underwear. The whole time, keep them on schedule and on task, simultaneously enforcing your unit's "no punching, no headlocks, no noogies" policy. Then as one final maneuver, Mom adjusts everybody's helmets (hair) to suit her, and you muster the troops to their appropriate assigned seating in the family's Armored Personnel Carrier.

Focus on "Know" more than on "No." It's become almost cliché that positive reinforcement is a more effective teaching technique than approaches designed simply to correct undesirable behaviors. The now-classic business book *Getting to Yes* taught sales techniques designed to break through the barriers that keep people from buying whatever it is you're selling. The key is genuine relationship. If you actually know each child—intimately—then you can pre-program them with good ideas about how they should behave, based upon their unique personalities. They'll *want* to behave well to please you if they actually *like* you. There's no doubt that children need you to set obvious boundaries for them. Making clear to your kids what you expect—and then equipping them to achieve that—is like building a huge fence all around your yard: You can send them out freely, without fear, knowing that they'll be safe, happy, successful human beings, protected from the influences of the outside world.

Lead and Inspire

Our kids pick up so much from us just as we do daily life together. Let your Christ-like example shine through in little ways just as much as in big ways. You know you shouldn't rob liquor stores. Don't drive over the speed limit, either, if that's something you don't want them to do. Cheerfully model the behavior that you want to infuse into them.

Just as with investing in your children, it will take time to plan and prepare some of the suggestions we offer here. Don't try to do everything all at once. Start small, and take advantage of "gaps" in your schedule by having a plan in advance that allows you to work on some of these things.

Develop a core of shared values. Where do these come from? Well, you'll need to write them, of course. We recommend coming up with 100 family values. Don't try to sit down and write them all at once. You'll never do that. Instead, take a notebook with you that you label "Family Values," and whenever one comes to you, or when you have a few minutes, jot it down. Spread it out over some time. Review the ones you've already written. Refine and revise when the mood strikes you.

Take care to structure your family's values so that the entire family will be able to embrace them. Then bring them up in appropriate settings as a means to guide your family's actions over time. For example, one of the Gunn Family Values is, "We do today what others won't, so we can have tomorrow what others can't":

My son says, "Dad, why do I have to study biology? Why do I need to know anything about the life cycle of an amoeba?"

And I can answer, "Son, remember: We do today what others won't—which is study and work hard—so that we can have tomorrow what others can't—which is straight A's. That's why you have to study your biology."

"Oh, yeah. I remember. That's true. Okay, dad."

Don't fear the teen years. I believe it was Mark Twain who once wrote, "When your child is 13, put them in a barrel and feed them through the knothole. When they turn 16, plug the hole." Isn't that how most people feel about their kids becoming teens? Why do we do that? You should build your family so that you're actually looking forward to the teen years. If you've transferred the family values and you've built the relationship, not only will your kids not want to do anything that disappoints you, they'll actually do everything they can to make you proud. We don't "do things for God" out of some sense of obligation or works, we serve Him joyfully because we love Him, and we're in a fulfilling, committed relationship. Model that same principle in your family, in your relationships with your children.

Perform family ministry together. Schedule planned, organized opportunities for your family to serve others together. Make a short list and go shopping together for groceries to give to a food bank. If your church offers short, local mission trips, sign up and take your kids. (Make sure in advance that they'll have age-appropriate opportunities to serve.) Even very little children can be taught how to plant flowers, and many senior centers offer opportunities for kids to just come "hang out" with residents. Take your kids and mow and edge a single mom's yard in your neighborhood. Help your kids bake something, and take it together to a retirement village community center. (No matter what you do, try to make it a habit to always call first and to ask for permission and any special instructions.)

Wednesday is our family day, so sometimes on Wednesdays we go to the dollar store and buy about sixty dollars' worth of items like gloves, socks, some candy, canned goods with peel-off lids, toothbrushes, and toothpaste. We'll go home, prepare ten sacks, and then drive around in a part of our city where we know a lot of homeless people hang out. We'll have the kids pray and ask God to reveal to us a person in need. When we find someone they feel strongly about, I'll jump out, run a sack out to the person, and tell them Jesus loves them and is looking out for them.

Sometimes we'll have the kids go through their things

together and fill several sacks with toys in good condition. We'll hop in the car and drive to a disadvantaged area of town, just as schools are letting out. We'll go to a school, hand a bag of toys to a kid on his way home, and tell him the Lord loves them and wants to bless him. Most kids usually light up and are very grateful. (How would it have made you feel growing up if someone just *handed* you a bag of toys?) It's a gift they weren't expecting, that they didn't deserve, that just happened to them: like grace.

Write encouraging notes. For each child, keep on a regular schedule of writing meaningful notes of encouragement to them. Avoid the temptation to look to these as teaching opportunities. Instead, focus on telling your child how great they are. Use their notes to help them see how their special talents, abilities, and God-given gifts make them unique. This may be one of those things that you need to put on your calendar, with reminders, as a task that you perform regularly.

In my family, I even often make a game out of finding the notes. For the younger kids, I'll hide the note in a room, and we'll play "hot and cold" until they find it. For the older kids, I'll strategically place their notes in bathroom drawers, on mirrors, in their car, or in a book that they're reading. If it's for a special occasion, I might even get them a card, place a note in it, and present it directly to them.

I recently read a touching story about a little girl whose parents discovered that she was dying of an inoperable brain tumor. They didn't tell her how serious it was because they didn't see any reason to frighten her or make her sad. She knew it was serious, and evidently she figured it out for herself, although she didn't let on. She lost her ability to speak, but she could still write. After several months, she passed away. When her parents were going through her things, they found a note from her to them and her little sister, a paper heart that she had cut out and written "I love you" to all of them. Then they continued to find her notes for months, tucked away in drawers and in cabinets, between books on the bookshelf, in the car. She was still speaking into their lives long after she was gone.

Write an encouraging letter on each child's birthday.

This is a great way to give your child a "state of the union" kind of historical measurement, a spiritual, psychological, and maturity meter, much like marks on a doorway measure their physical growth over time. Use these letters to mark the milestone improvements that you've seen take place in that child's life during the previous year. Single out accomplishments and growth that you've noticed. Express excitement and cast vision for their upcoming year. Be sure you leave yourself enough advance time to do these letters justice. Some—perhaps most—of your children will collect and keep their letters, cherishing them over a lifetime. One day, your grandkids and great grandkids may even be reading them. Keep the audience in mind as you write. What do you want to say to them?

Pray together before bedtime. The simplest way to is to go in as a couple and pray with each child or group of children as part of your "tuck-in" ritual. Or, you might want to call everyone together, say, in the living room, before bed and pray as a family. If you pray all together, stand in a circle and hold hands.

No matter what approach you use, model honest prayer for your children. Pray the same way with them that you pray by yourself. Express praise and thanks to God for things He's done for your family, and ask for things you need, as well as for Him to change you according to His will.

A friend of mine told me about an old acrostic he learned in the Baptist church as a child: PRAY:

Praise – Thank God for what he's done.

Repent — Ask for forgiveness.

Another — Pray for someone else's need.

Yourself — Ask for whatever you need.

Be sure you give each child the opportunity to pray individually. As you tuck them in to bed, encourage them to continue talking to God after you've left the room, as they're drifting off to sleep. You can pray specific things for individual children or general things for the entire family. Really, the possibilities are infinite. Do what works for your family. Just set the spiritual standard for your household.

Use the "listening baton." Sometimes it's difficult to talk through sensitive subjects without seeing the conversation devolve into an argument. When a disagreement breaks out between children, the best way to get the whole story is to give each child the opportunity to share "their side," uninterrupted. For these times, we use a physical, actual small baton—like the kind runners hand off in a relay. Only one person at a time is permitted to speak: whoever is holding the baton. They get to say their peace, and then, once they're completely finished, they hand off the baton for the next person's turn.

Doing it this way makes total honesty much more likely, since all the witnesses are present; each child knows that the whole story is going to come out anyway, whether they or a sibling choose to share it. We also find it useful to have each person speak just a little, and then allow the other person involved to paraphrase back to them what they've just said. This forces both parties to focus on what's being said, rather than getting lost in their own thoughts. True communication happens, helping each person feel that they're truly being heard and understood.

(Bonus! This technique works equally well between spouses.)

Practice a weekly family devotion (at least). Some high-achieving Type-A dads will strive for a daily devotion right off the bat. If that's you, more power to you! You go, Dad! Just consider: While a daily devotion is a great method of self-discipline, if you try to impose that same thing on your family, your tendency may be to make it more legalistic and "check the box" than a true, high-impact opportunity for life change.

If just the thought of a family devotion makes your heart race and your palms sweaty, shoot for a goal of just once a week. You're far more likely to succeed, and you can grow the frequency organically over time, if that fits your family's needs. The reason we say "at least" is because consistency will be critical to making this stick.

Don't try to over-spiritualize it, either. Give some thought to what the members of your family are actually going through (illness, financial difficulty, an impending move, fear of the dark, etc.), study that in the Scriptures, and present them with truth they can apply right now. Demonstrate a commitment to divining the truth from God's word and allowing it to guide your lives. Teach them that the Bible is full of God's love letters, left for us to discover. Don't neglect the work of God in you...and in your family.

Memorize weekly verses. You can coordinate these with your family devotions, or you can set unrelated targets for individual children. Make the verses you select age-appropriate. Older children will be able to handle more sophisticated and longer verses, while younger children will require shorter verses in easier translations. It's critical that they don't memorize just for the sake of memorizing. Take the time to make sure each child understands what they're learning, and why. For example, 2 Timothy 1:7, "For God gave us a spirit not of fear but of power and love and self-control" (ESV) is a great verse for a child suffering through nightmares, fear of dogs, fear of the dark, etc.

Consider implementing a system of rewards to encourage your kids, such as points that they can trade in for material things (toys or games) or special treats (ice cream) or special outings (taking that child to a ball game or ballet). Schedule a regular rewards "ceremony" where each child gets a turn to show off their progress (with the rest of the family cheering them on). You could even make it a special segment of weekly Family Night.

As with the other spiritual aspects of family life, Dad should set the standard. The best way you can keep your kids encouraged is to learn the verses yourself and playfully drill them throughout the week. Don't make it competition; reinforce that you're a team who helps each other. Make it as much your responsibility as theirs.

Admit when you're wrong, and ask for forgiveness when you make mistakes. People sometimes ask me why I seem to talk about this so much. Well, it's because it's so important. Modeling humility for your family is the best way they'll get it. Learn to say, "Honey, I was wrong. I don't deserve your forgiveness, but would you please forgive me?" It teaches them the behavior you hope they'll have, while at the same time drawing them closer to you in love.

This is a great way for you to model humility and honesty for your children. You're human, so you're going to mess up—at least every once in a while. And if you don't believe you will, then you're just proving my point: "Pride goes before destruction, a haughty spirit before a fall. (Proverbs 16:18) Seriously, if you lose your temper, if you overspend, if you struggle with impatience or anxiety, be real. Your kids are going to see it anyway. You can teach them how to foster healthy, transparent relationships, simply by being authentic yourself. Of course, keep your disclosures age-appropriate, and don't frighten your children needlessly. Don't say things like: "Kids, Daddy's afraid the bank's going to take our house."

Certainly you can communicate even difficult things in a spirit of peace and teachable moments. Model 1 Thessalonians 5:16 for them: "Therefore confess your sins to each other and pray for each other so that you may be healed." Besides getting comfortable asking for forgiveness, follow up with, "Would you pray with me?" As that verse continues, your prayer with them will be "powerful and effective." Isn't that a great promise? You can teach your kids to pray powerfully and effectively!

Take the lead on children's bed and bath times. I was tempted to say "help with" instead of "take the lead on," but that's not really what I mean. If you simply "help" or "participate," that implies that Mom's doing all the work, and you're just standing there, "supervising" like a government employee. A close friend was telling me that he mentioned to an older gentleman he worked with that he had changed a dirty diaper, and the old-school guy became indignant: "Why would you change a diaper?! That's disgusting!" He considered it "woman's work."

Ephesians 5:25 makes it clear that how we love our wives is by laying down our lives for them. You're not really "loving her as yourself" or "honoring her over yourself" by taking advantage of her as your nanny and maid. As with other tasks related to your children, explore Mom's comfort level, and let the things you do serve her. Don't rob her if she feels these responsibilities are God's gift to her.

Get as involved in your kids' lives as you can. Your interest in their lives communicates clearly to them that you care about them, that you love them.

Give Your Kids a Voice

What follows is a questionnaire (also available on our website) that you can give to your children. It's a simple way you can have your children offer you straightforward feedback about how you're doing. Imagine if your boss gave you the chance to honestly tell him how he's doing! It's a risk, but it demonstrates that you really care. It's the least you can do for your kids.

We would like to have your honest answers to these questions. Please tell us how you really feel, not what you think we want to hear.

How important do you feel? Write a "+" if you feel more important than what is listed, a "-" is you feel less important, and "=" if you feel as important as what is listed.

To my dad, I feel more or less important than… His work ___ his tools ___ his friends ___ his rest, recreation ___ his car ___ his relationship with Mom ___ his relationship with God ___ his yard ___ the church ___ outside activities or meetings___

I would feel more important to my dad if he would…

I feel really proud of myself when I…

To my mom, I feel more or less important than… Her work ___ her house ___ her friends ___ her rest, recreation ___ her clothes ___ her relationship with Dad ___ her relationship with God ___ her kitchen ___ the church ___ outside activities or meetings___

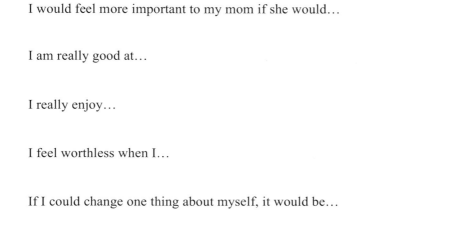

I would feel more important to my mom if she would…

I am really good at…

I really enjoy…

I feel worthless when I…

If I could change one thing about myself, it would be…

Start Today… As we said at the beginning, don't beat yourself up over the things you haven't done. Most people, as you begin to implement some of what we suggest in this chapter, will begin to discover all kinds of different ways that you can love your family afresh and anew. Don't hold back. Start small. Do what you can do today. When you see the results, it will encourage you to keep adding. Don't put it off. Start today.

Chapter 9: Do Not Give Up!

I mentioned before how I spent most of my adult life as a lukewarm follower if Christ. It's not that I was never hot, it's that I averaged being lukewarm. I was like an electric lamp with a 100 watt bulb in it. Once or twice a week I would be plugged in, and then I was hot. The light of Jesus would shine brightly out of every pore for a day or two, and then I would cool off for a while. When I talk about this at our Family-iD events, I have a real lamp on stage with me and ask someone from the audience come up on stage. I plug in the lamp, then unplug it after a few seconds. I plug it in and then back out about four times. I ask my helper to touch the bulb. Even though it was white hot a few seconds ago, now it's barely warm. I ask a simple question, "How do I keep the bulb hot?" Their answer, "Keep it plugged in!"

In our spiritual life we call it "staying connected to the vine". When I was forty-two years old, I was fed up with my roller-coaster relationship with God. I decided I was going to do whatever I had to do to stay connected every day.

My oldest daughter Hannah turned out to be the one who helped keep me accountable in the beginning. I told her I was going to read my Bible, pray, and journal every morning for six weeks. To help keep myself focused, I told her I would give her $200.00 and clean her room for a month if I missed one day. The $200.00 would sting and there was no way I was going to be making her bed for the next thirty days. I started with the book of James in the New Testament. I got up early, before anyone else was awake, made myself a cup of coffee, and would sit in my favorite chair with my Bible, a pen and my journal. I would simply read until something in the scripture spoke to me. Sometimes I would read several paragraphs and other times a few verses before something resonated. Then I would write that thought down in my journal. After that I would write out a prayer to God ending in the name of Jesus.

I did it! I stayed connected to the vine every day for six weeks and did not have to clean Hannah's room for a month.

It's been 8 years and with a few exceptions due to illness or travel, I have remained connected to the vine.

I am not going to be one of these people who tells you that life became "all roses and no thorns" or "all cherries and no pits". The truth is, the enemy does not want you to be connected to the vine. He also doesn't want you to have the type of family this book is about. If I had not been connected to the vine every day for the past five years, I would have given up in many areas of my life. My friend Craig Groeschel once said, "The higher you go in your spiritual walk, the bigger the demons get!" You may have heard people say "God won't allow anything into your life that you can't handle." That's a misinterpretation of 1 Corinthians 10:13 which says, "No temptation has seized you except what is common to man. And God is faithful; he will not let you be tempted beyond what you can bear. But when you are tempted, he will also provide a way out so that you can stand up under it." This verse is not talking about problems in life, it's talking about the temptations of sin. The point of being connected to the vine every day is that I am not trying to handle all the problems myself. I am turning them over to God every day, sometimes every hour and every minute. I have a peace and joy in my life that is hard to explain to the average person and at the same time I have experienced challenges that have been very difficult on my family. In the past three years I have been falsely accused of a civil crime and found guilty. My wife and I were so confident I was going to be acquitted, we took our home-schooled children to court with us for an education. We had no idea the opposing attorneys would flat make stuff up and call me all kinds of evil names. I ended up losing the case, my life savings, the business I had built for thirty years and the trust of many friends. We were also saddled with a half-million dollars in legal fees and fines.

I went through a tough time, but my heavenly daddy reached down and held my hand as I reached up and He is walking me to the other side. I wouldn't trade any part of my journey. My relationship with Rhonda is better than ever. My kids were able to watch their daddy hold God's hand as he went through a fire. The process also helped me realize I was too focused on money and financial independence. My dependence is now where it needs to be, daily focused on my Lord and Savior Jesus Christ.

THE SIX WEEK COMMITMENT

Every time we do a Family-iD Weekend event, I go into detail of my own journey staying connected to the vine. I challenge every person in the auditorium to make a six week commitment like the one I did with my daughter almost a decade ago.

I challenge you in the same way right now. I mean RIGHT NOW! Find someone who will hold you accountable. Tell that person you will eat a can of dog-food if you miss one day, or whatever will motivate you stay focused on the goal. Go to a bookstore and buy an empty book (a journal) and start filling it up. (or go to my website www.GregGunn.com and sign up for our online journal.) I now have several volumes of my conversations with God. Make it simple for yourself like I did, no pressure with the amount or the quality of your journal entries. Just consistent words from God. Choose a book of the bible and start reading until something speaks to your heart, then write a brief reflection on His words and your prayers about whatever is on your mind. I often write the specific verses in my journal, then comment on them and then pray.

To help you get started, a few of us at Family-iD ministries wrote and published a six-week workbook to help you get kick-started. If you attend one of our events, you can buy one for two bucks. If you can't make it to an event, we scanned the workbook and made it available for free as a PDF file on our website. You can find it under the resources tab at www.GregGunn.com. You can print the whole thing at once and put it in a 3-ring binder, or print one day at a time as you move forward. I never knew I would have had so much fun. So will you. You can also buy a hard copy on Amazon.com. Just search "Greg C. Gunn" and "Connecting to the Vine". The cost is only about six dollars.

Expect trials when you start and from now on!

We in the United States of America are spoiled. We have enjoyed almost a century of wealth and opportunity. We have heard all kinds of tele-evangelists give us a version of the Gospel that is far from truth. This "gospel" tells us if we follow Jesus and have faith; we will be healthy, wealthy and wise.

We have been told we were boarding a Christian Cruise when we joined. Wrong! This is where we need to revisit the words of a great old hymn:

Onward, Christian Soldiers

Onward, Christian soldiers, marching as to war,
With the cross of Jesus going on before.
Christ, the royal Master, leads against the foe;
Forward into battle see His banners go!
At the sign of triumph Satan's host doth flee;
On then, Christian soldiers, on to victory!
Hell's foundations quiver at the shout of praise;
Brothers, lift your voices, loud your anthems raise.
Like a mighty army moves the church of God;
Brothers, we are treading where the saints have trod.
We are not divided, all one body we,
One in hope and doctrine, one in charity.
Crowns and thrones may perish, kingdoms rise and wane,
But the church of Jesus constant will remain.
Gates of hell can never 'gainst that church prevail;
We have Christ's own promise, and that cannot fail.
Onward then, ye people, join our happy throng,
Blend with ours your voices in the triumph song.
Glory, laud, and honor unto Christ the King,
This through countless ages men and angels sing.

We didn't board a cruise ship, we boarded a battleship!

As soon as you take a stand for righteousness in any area of your life you will discover new conflicts and problems you never imagined.

I like what Mother Teresa once said, "I call my failures

and problems 'Kisses of Jesus'; when they enter my life, they cause me to run into the arms of my Lord and Savior."

We should all have that same attitude toward the challenges we face. We are His children and He is our Daddy. We don't expect our children to live lives with no problems. We also expect our children to bring their problems to us and let us help them bare the burdens of living.

When you get discouraged, (and you will) remember all relationships take time. Some days you feel good about your relationship with God and other days you feel a thousand miles away.

I remember a story about an old married farm couple. Their main vehicle was a pickup truck for many years. Early in their marriage, they would both get in on the driver's side. They sat so close to each other, they looked like one person while driving down the road. As the years went by, they both entered from opposite sides and each had their own door arm rest. One morning as they were heading into town the wife complained that they weren't as close as they used to be in the truck. The farmer looked over at her and said, "I didn't move!"

We are often in the same situation in our relationship with God. We move away from him and then complain about how far away we are from him.

Stay in the game. Stay connected to the vine. Allow God to be a part of your life on every level. Don't give up!

Chapter 10: The Legacy of Sarah Jane Diffee

In 1908, Joe Diffee lived with his wife Sarah Jane and their eight children in Caddo Gap, Arkansas. Caddo Gap was a tiny town about 40 miles west of Hot Springs, known throughout Montgomery County, Arkansas, for three things: gambling, bootleg liquor, and prostitution. The Diffees were close family friends with another couple who had eight kids of their own, the Votts. The Vott children and the Diffee children were close in age; most having a corresponding child only a month or so different in age from them, so they were all best friends.

Joe's grandmother had handed down to him a recipe for granular laundry soap. At the time, most soaps were still made in the traditional way, based in oils and fats. This meant they didn't break down well in water, so they weren't very good at cleaning fabrics. Experimenting through trial and error, Joe's grandmother invented a unique blend that played nicely with water and was ideal for clothes. She called it Sunshine Soap. One of her secrets was ground up peach leaves, which had the brilliant whitening effects of bleach, but without the harsh, chemical side effects.

Although Joe's primary vocation in Caddo Gap had been as a farmer/rancher, he traveled all over the country, using his inherited formula to try to get a soap factory business rolling, signing up investors as franchisees.

For years Joe traveled, selling soap. While Sarah Jane was at home trying to raise her children, a friend invited her to a brush arbor revival meeting. Even though she had surrendered her life to Christ at the age of 14 and married at 16, because there was not one church in the town of Caddo Gap, her faith had begun to wane; she felt that something was missing. The first night there, Sarah Jane received the infilling of the Holy Spirit, with a renewed thirst for truth and hope, she continued attending the meetings night after night, all eight kids in tow. Sarah Jane arranged to visit with the evangelist holding the revival, and she asked his advice about how she could raise a family of Christ-followers in a town where prostitution and gambling were considered reputable businesses. The evangelist told her about Vilonia, Arkansas, a small town about 130 miles away, where a Christian school had been started by a group of radical Methodists in 1900. In 1905, they had even expanded the school to include a college, Arkansas Holiness College. Vilonia sounded like Eden to Sarah Jane, but of course she had no way of getting there. The evangelist felt the Holy Spirit leading him to give her $20, so if she could get her family to Hot Springs, Ark. she would have enough to buy a train ticket from Hot Springs to Vilonia.

When Joe returned, he was surprised to learn of his wife's newfound Christian zeal. When she told him what she wanted to do and that the evangelist had given her the money, he was shocked. He told her plainly: "there is only one reason a man would give a woman $20.00 in this town." So "You can move if you want, but my kids are staying right here in Caddo Gap with me." She told him that if he tried to stop her, she'd swear before a judge that none of those kids were his. In a town like Caddo Gap, and with a husband who was away traveling most of the time, Joe recognized his position, and relented.

Sarah Jane and the kids said their tearful goodbyes to the Votts, then struck out by wagon, headed for Hot Springs. They carried everything they could with them, planning to buy their train tickets once they got there. A little frustrated and still confused, Joe stayed behind. Sarah Jane and the children only made it 20 miles that first night, about halfway. Afraid and exhausted, they unloaded their belongings on the side of the road and tried to get comfortable enough to sleep. At midnight they were awakened by the sound of someone coming into their camp, it was Joe, scaring them half to death he showed up on horseback. The next, day he took his family the rest of the way himself.

They decided to make Vilonia the base of operations. As the children grew up and married, they would join the ever increasing-soap business. This venture would end up carrying them all over the country, even some parts of Canada. By the early 1920's, the business took Joe to California. In a place called Signal Hill, north of Long Beach, he found an ideal location for one of his soap factories. He was able to buy the land, but he was going to need to draw on money he had saved in banks in Arkansas for everything else. When his bankers refused to wire him his money, he began to worry about its safety, and with his health failing, he was forced to travel all the way back home to retrieve it in person.

Before he left, he needed to secure some reliable transportation, low on funds Joe decided to trade the Signal Hill property in California for a Model T. Ford. Just a short time later, in 1921, oil was discovered there. Ultimately, one of the richest oil fields in the world; it produced over 1 billion barrels of oil by 1984. The field is still active and produced over 1.5 million barrels of oil in 2002 alone. Joe Diffee had missed out on a fortune. In 1923, Joe died suddenly at the age of 60 of a kidney disease. With the founder and driving force of the company dead, his oldest son Walter secretly sold his patents for Sunshine Soap to a corporate buyer for an undisclosed amount. That buyer was Procter and Gamble. No one knows how much he got, or where all the money went, but needless to say nobody remembers seeing or hearing much from Walter again. Joe Diffee had missed out on a second fortune.

The Diffee family settled in Vilonia, and managed to get all eight of their children into the Arkansas Holiness School. Through their studies and their mother's influence, each child became a follower of Christ. They each met and married someone connected to the school. John C. Diffee married Laura Gray. His brother Roy married Rev. Agnes, who became the Pastor of one of the largest churches in the country, Little Rock First Church. Her radio program became one of the most listened-to religious programs in the southwest. In 1930, the Depression brought hard times to Arkansas Holiness College, so in 1931 it merged with the Bethany-Peniel College in Bethany, Oklahoma, to survive. Bethany-Peniel would later become one of the founding colleges of what is today Southern Nazarene University, still in Bethany, Oklahoma. John and Laura had 7 children as each of them got married or went off to school they seem to gravitate to Bethany. Each of the Diffee kids married Christian spouses and, as the younger ones went off to school, John and Laura Diffee followed them to Oklahoma in 1954.

The Votts, who they had left behind in Caddo Gap, did not fare so well. Some were taken by alcohol; some by disease, even some by prostitution, and one was shot in the street by a jealous husband. Each of the eight Vott children died before the age of 40. Even Mrs. Vott lost her life in a single-car accident. She was alone, and she had been drinking heavily.

In 1954, John Diffee, the 4th of the eight Diffee children, founded Diffee Motor Company with his youngest son, Vic Diffee, selling cars now for over 55years. In 1991, Vic and his sons opened, a second Diffee Motors location in El Reno, Oklahoma. Their advertisements tout the "Diffee Family Difference". They remain in business today and both have the 4th and 5th generations involved in the family business.

The first time I can remember spending time with Sarah Jane Diffee was in 1968, when I was 8 years old. It was her 102nd birthday. You see, Sarah Jane was my great-grandmother. John Diffee, her son who started the car business, was my grandfather. When I was still just a little boy, My Aunt Jane Krutz told my mother that Sarah Jane prayed for each of her 74+ children, grandchildren and great-grandchildren by name every day. She prayed...for me. In her later life, as her sight began to fail her, she devoted herself to prayer and time alone with her Savior; she had so passionately loved for over 90 years. Grandma Diffee asked her precious Jesus to save each of us, and to make sure we each had a relationship with him. Sarah Jane left to be with him in 1972, at 106 years old.

In the late 1980's , my Uncle Vic Diffee returned to Caddo Gap, Arkansas, to see what had become of my ancestors' Egypt. He reported back that it was still there, but just barely. Most of the buildings are either gone or boarded up and condemned. There's no industry, and few people. The one business he found in the center of town that was still open was the little convince store that had recently been converted into an adult bookstore. That's the legacy of Caddo Gap's choices over the last four generations. As it turned out, it was more like Sodom and Gomorrah than like Egypt.

Sarah Jane Diffee's 100-year story is now in my hands, mine and my cousins. It is a story of courage, integrity, faith, discipline, diligence, hard work and sacrifice that has yielded eternal gain, changing the lives of literally hundreds of people, forever. My great-grandfather Joe almost gained the whole world—twice—but it very likely may have cost him his soul. It most certainly would have cost him his children. So now Grandma Diffee's 100-year story passes to me. I have big shoes to fill. Will I make the right choices? Will I lead others to lay the foundation for many Godly generations who will follow them? As my own light fades, will I pray for each of my great-grandchildren by name every day, alone in my room with my sweet Savior? I believe that everything happening today, God had set in motion 100 years ago, and everything that God wants to do 100 years from now He is preparing for right now. That is why, I believe so much of what is happening in our world today, seems to make no sense.

What's your 100-year story? Do you have a Grandma Diffee in your ancestry? Or are you that person? You know, the next great pastor or evangelist i.e. Billy Graham or Billy Sunday, may come from your family. The person who cures cancer or AIDS may be one of your children, your grandchildren, your great-grandchildren. A perpetual motion machine, a boundless clean energy source, may come out of your family. It doesn't matter where you started. Just cast a vision, write it down, it will resonate in your children's DNA if not, it's not meant for them, or its not meant for this generation, it might be for the next generation, but only you can cast that vision. We all have vision leak, keep casting. The choice, the opportunity—the future…is yours.

Write it down…

…Live it out…

Pass it on!

What is your 100 year story? Go to www.greggunn.com and share with us your story. I can't wait to hear about how you are going to change the world! We can't do it alone and we are not supposed to, so let's connect; I can't do it without you, and you can't do it without me.

Greg C. Gunn

Made in the USA
San Bernardino, CA
02 February 2014